A Sport
Psychology
Workbook
for Riders

A Sport Psychology Workbook for Riders

ANN S. REILLY, Ph. D.

J.A. ALLEN

LONDON

British Library Cataloguing in Publication Data
A catalogue record for this book is available from the British Library

ISBN 0.85131.771.5

Published in Great Britain in 2000 by
J. A. Allen
An imprint of Robert Hale Ltd.
Clerkenwell House, 45–47 Clerkenwell Green,
London, EC1R OH7

Photographs property of the author, except for the following provided by and reproduced
with permission of, their owners: page 4 by Richard Sullivan, pages 6, 101 by John Irving
Stevenson, page 28 by Christine and Ted Tchir (Sport Horse Studio), pages 14,41,124 by
Theresa Ramsay, pages 86–7 by Robert Stevenson, page 112 by Jane Hitchen.
Front cover: Mary Lou Marvin (top right), Bob Langrish (bottom right).

Colour separation by Tenon & Polert Colour Scanning Ltd
Printed by Dah Hua Printing Press Co. Ltd., Hong Kong

Contents

Contents

List of Photographs

Acknowledgements

First, many thanks to Mary Coker, Lois Vitt and the late Jacqueline Kennedy Onassis for inspiring me to write this book. For your beautiful photos – thank you Janet Hitchen, Theresa Ramsay, Robert Stevenson, Richard Sullivan and Ted Tchir.

Martin Diggle deserves a huge thank-you for editing this book, as does J.A. Allen for publishing it.

Last but not least, thanks to Robert J. Rotella, Ph.D. for teaching me sport psychology, my clients for teaching me even more, my long-time teacher Kathy Doyle Newman and Gerry and Katherine for your unconditional advice and support, my family and parents – Michael and Nancy Reilly – for your love, support and patience, and to all the horses who have helped teach me the sport as well as psychology!

1

Winning the Mind Game

As a rider, you have the choice to think like a winner or think like a loser. You are the only person in the universe who has the power to take control of your mind and emotions. In this book, ideas and exercises that train the mind and body for peak performance are presented for you to work through. They will teach you to believe that, when you take charge of yourself, your potential is limitless. Thus, mental training can open up a new avenue to enjoyment of riding.

Truly great, successful riders have developed attitudes, motivational tendencies, self-confidence, and the ability to visualize success that set them apart from others. I have seen people make dramatic changes in their riding and in other parts of their life by using this system. It is very simple: a matter of developing the attitudes and beliefs by which you give yourself *permission* to be successful. The self-confidence develops from learning to rely on your inner self and thus attract the horses, people, and experiences you need. Changes in self-concept occur from learning to see yourself and the world in a way that is enriching. With your new attitude, you will focus on the belief that you can create whatever you desire.

Affirmation: I am able to create my reality. I can obtain what I want and need to grow as a rider.

The world is an abundant and prosperous place. The mind is very powerful. When it is focused, with an established, positive belief in yourself and your abilities, you will be able to visualize the greatness that is inside you. You will see that dreams can be brought to reality. This book will teach you, step-by-step, how to transform your dreams into realities.

Affirmation: I am now creating magical moments when I ride. One moment blossoms into another, and another, and another – into infinity.

Do you ever wonder why some of the most successful riders in the world are not necessarily the brightest, most talented, or best trained? What do these people know that others do not about success? They have learned to see themselves as winners, and learned how to use the mind in a way that creates success. They are able to tune out their doubts, focus on their goals, successfully overcome obstacles or distractions and see their goals attained. They may not know each step of the way analytically, but they have the belief and trust that they will get to where they want to be at some point in time. They commit each day to doing something, big or small, that brings them closer to their goals.

By making the commitment to work through the exercises in this book, a little each day, you are making the commitment to unleash the winner inside yourself!

Questionnaire: Self-perception

1. Do you view yourself as a winner?

   What are the characteristics that make you a winner?

2. What reasons do you have for not viewing yourself as a winner?

A winner's determination is evident as Gerry Newman prepares for another victory at the Middleburg Spring Steeplechase races.

Are you willing to give up those thoughts and beliefs?

3. Do you view yourself as a competent rider? Why or why not?

2

Peak Performance

What exactly is peak performance? It is the feeling of performing at your best, without apparent effort. The following quotation explains the experience:

> I walked into the ring and the ground felt very soft. I almost felt one with my horse – like I could feel every beat of his canter. The ring looked a little bigger, but everything was flowing and effortless. I did not have to think about where I was going. I did not worry about seeing my distances, they were just there for me and I could really feel the horse jumping – every movement. I guess it felt like watching a slow motion video, but I just went with it and did not try to speed things up because everything was right there and felt great. I was really riding and not worrying about anything. No tension, no negative thoughts, just riding my best.

This rider is describing riding 'in the zone'. The rider was so involved in the activity that nothing else seemed to matter. Being 'in the zone' is the ultimate in being totally engrossed in what you are doing. It is an incredible feeling! If you have ever experienced it, you will know what I am talking about. You can train for this experience by learning about the characteristics of peak performance and practising those characteristics when schooling and performing. It happens when you trust yourself and your horse enough to perform on automatic pilot. The characteristics are:

- Loss of fear – no fear of failure.
- No conscious thinking of performance.
- Total immersion in the activity (focus in the present).
- Narrow focus of attention.
- Effortless performance – not forcing it.
- Feeling of being in complete control (because you are riding in the present, which is all that you can control).
- Time/space disorientation (things usually seem slowed down).
- Universe perceived to be integrated and unified.
- Unique, temporary, involuntary experience.

(Ravizza, 1977)

Robert Stevenson, seen here representing Canada at the 1992 Olympics on *Risky Business*, used sport psychology to get 'in the zone'.

Questionnaire: Best Performances

1. Think about your best performance ever. How did your mind and body feel?

   List what your thoughts were.

   Focus on what your energy level was.

   How did you prepare for that performance?

2. Think of your worst performance – how did your body feel?

   List your thoughts.

3. List the differences between the two: how did they differ?

THE PEAK PERFORMANCE CURVE

Research has discovered that there is a peak performance zone. When you are in that zone your performance is maximized: your mind and body have just the right amount of energy and intensity to perform the task well. The diagram below depicts peak performance in relation to level of arousal.

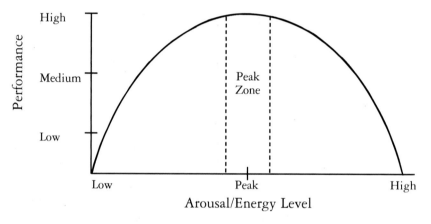

The Peak Performance Curve (Oxendine 1970)

Think of the arousal level as the amount of mental and physical energy or intensity that you and your horse need to put in a good performance. You must also match your mental and physical energy and intensity to the requirements of the performance. Riding a dressage test or other flatwork may require less energy than riding cross-country. Learning to prepare yourself and your horse for peak performance in any sphere requires awareness and some trial and error. Once you learn what is best for you and your horse, the key is preparing yourself that way for each performance. Since there is variability in your mental and physical state and your horse's from day to day, it takes awareness and effort to psych up or calm down to the level at which you perform well.

To do this, you need to be able to read your own mind and body and also assess your horse's, and then ride the horse that you have under you. I often hear riders complaining because their horse did not feel right. The solution to the problem is to focus in the present, determine 'where the horse is' each day and then devise a plan for getting him to perform well. If you are feeling too nervous or too lazy, first do what it takes to get yourself psyched down or psyched up. Then get on and prepare your horse.

If, when you mount, your horse feels lazy because it is a hot summer day, practise psyching up as if you were competing on that day. Think goal, think energy, use your leg to psych up your horse and get him to carry you. Alternatively, if your horse is strong, do what it takes to work him down to the level where you need him to be to perform well. Then do the same when you are competing. Allow yourself enough time to prepare your horse so that he can perform to his best. Also, allow yourself the time to do what you need to do to prepare yourself mentally.

Reviewing the peak performance curve, riding a dressage test may require riders to be a little 'left of centre', which means a relaxed mind with a narrow focus of attention, less physical energy, and less of the 'pumped up' feeling. For a major showjumping course, or a cross-country course, the rider may want to be a little 'right of centre' – more physical energy whilst maintaining a relaxed, focused mind. Essentially, the rider must feel able to concentrate on the requirements of the performance, with mind and body working on the performance in a flowing manner; so there is synchronicity with the movements of the horse, and enough energy to complete the performance. Practise this each time you ride – just as if you were performing on that day.

RIDE TO WIN

Confident, focused riders have a plan and ride to execute that plan. Their focus on the present allows them to concentrate and react appropriately to changes in their horse or changes in the conditions

Gerry Newman dismissed this error and went on to win the race.

or requirements of the course or race. *A key to riding in the present is developing the ability to accept and dismiss immediately any mistakes or errors made while performing.* This prevents being distracted by something that happened in the past, which you can do nothing about. For example, if your horse is showing an incorrect bend to the right while you are riding a dressage test, you need to focus on the correction and riding the test, rather than on the wrong bend itself. The mistake many riders make, especially in competition, is that they focus on the problem and thereby freeze, and are thus unable to make the correction.

Less confident riders often let self-criticism, fear, or doubt distract them from focusing in the present. Margo, an FEI-level dressage rider, often let self-criticism distract her attention from the present. Despite popular belief, self-critical, fearful or doubtful thoughts rarely enhance performance. They usually cause guilt, blame, shame, frustration, or anger, and these emotional responses tend to hinder peak performance by tying riders up in knots. When Margo felt her horse resist, make a mistake, or disobey her aids, she would immediately become self-critical and then become angry. She would think that she was a low-level rider because her horse was misbehaving, and instead of focusing on accepting and correcting the disobedience or mistake, she would become emotional. Often the memory of a bad experience or mistake caused Margo to panic, which in turn caused her horse to panic. When Margo learned to stop criticizing herself, to forget the past and accept that getting involved in the process meant riding through the rough spots whilst focusing on the goal, she began frequently to experience rides, both in practice and in the show ring, where she was totally in the 'zone'; into the process so much that nothing, internal or external, distracted her. She often felt so confident and focused that her performance felt effortless.

Hints for Developing a Positive Focus

- Focus on mastering the basics – pace, rhythm, balance, and straightness.
- From the moment you sit in the saddle, try to focus on feeling one stride at a time. You can do this with your eyes closed also.
- On a daily basis, practise visualizing what you want to happen. When your thoughts become negative, immediately change them to focusing on what you want to achieve. (See Chapter 8.)
- On paper, identify the steps entailed in the process you are involved in. You can break the process down into long-term, intermediate, and short-term goals. If you do not know what is involved in the process of reaching goals, ask advice from someone who has successfully been where you want to go.
- Watch others who perform the way that you want to perform. Try to avoid watching others who perform poorly. You want to watch what you want to happen!

In the chapters that follow you will learn how to develop a positive focus.

SKILL DEVELOPMENT AND PEAK PERFORMANCE

Learning a skill and being able to perform that skill automatically are two different things. There is a lot of variability in performance when learning a skill. As the skill becomes second nature, the variability tends to decrease, although there are some times when performance drops (slumps) and some when performance peaks higher than ever before.

When skills become automatic, riders no longer need to think about execution. Since the mind does not need to focus on execution it may shift to focusing on negative thoughts about not being able to execute the skills competently. It is at this time that riders need to learn to trust what they have learned and focus on relaxation and flow, pace, balance, feel and straightness.

Fatigue and Peak Performance

Have you ever wondered why your performance is often better after a break? While you are practising and competing on a daily basis, mental and physical fatigue build up; the fatigue goes away during a break and you subsequently perform better. This is because while fatigue is building up, it does not allow you to perform at your best. The improvement in performance after a break is called 'spontaneous recovery' and is a well-established phenomenon of the learning process.

3

Focusing in the Present

When riding in the 'zone', the rider's focus of attention is in the present moment and the mind is free from self-critical or judgemental thoughts about performance: the rider is 'just doing it'. Riding in the present allows riders to concentrate and focus their attention on the performance; to feel in control and enjoy the performance, without feeling as if they have to force or control it.

When your trainer says 'concentrate', what he or she really means is *pay attention to the process*. Feel the horse underneath you and make the appropriate adjustments so that you have the proper pace, balance, straightness, and intensity. Focusing involves paying attention to what is happening in the present moment; concentrating on the technical requirements of the task at hand. Worrying about something that occurred in the past, or thoughts about what may occur in the future, distract riders from focusing on what is happening in the present. It is common to find riders who focus on the buck; the shy; the stop; the possibility of forgetting the course; their horse not liking a jump; how well they may or may not perform, or on only one aspect of the competition, such as the cross-country phase or a special class. The mental error here is that, when they are focused on what they do not want to happen, they often create an expectancy of its occurrence. In other words, they make the error happen. The key is to focus on the goal of the whole performance.

ATTAINING POSITIVE FOCUS

As you are preparing to ride each day, assess what you are thinking about. Are your thoughts centred on what you are doing at that moment, or on something else? Tell yourself to focus on what you are

Riding long hunter courses can challenge one's ability to focus in the present. Eyes up and staying in the rhythm keep the author and *Bye Farr* flowing in the present.

doing each moment. When you are riding, focus on how each stride feels under you. That will focus you in the present and centre you. The key to riding well is riding each stride, keeping the horse balanced and flowing.

Questionnaire: Are You Focused in the Present?

1. Do you find yourself day-dreaming more about the future than paying attention to what is happening in the present?

2. When you arrive at a competition do you find yourself thinking only about going into the ring to perform, or about results, rather than focusing on the process that brings you to your performance?

3. Do you frequently find yourself wishing you were doing something else, or at some other place?

4. Are you able to focus on the present stride, or are you distracted by what happened before that stride or what will happen in a few strides time?

5. When preparing for competition, do you think more about what could go wrong than actually preparing, and then panic at the last minute when you are not ready to go?

If the answer to any or all of these questions is 'yes', it is an indication that work on focusing in the present will help your performance. You will find that when you are focused in the present, on the pace, balance, feel and straightness, you have a clear mind and achieve more.

4

From Negative to Positive

I recall volunteering to act as a collecting ring steward at a local show. A young rider, on her pony, was hanging around the arena entrance. She was not pleased with her performance in the first round. I asked her what was wrong, and she said: 'I don't like the second course and I did not do well the first time'. I encouraged her to change her attitude towards the course. I told her that her chances for a good ride would be much better if she liked the course. Then I broke it down for her, and talked her through it a few times. We discussed the possible problems that could arise and how she would handle them. She then said she did not think the course was so bad. She went into the ring and had a very good ride. I then overheard her mother, who had no idea who I was or that I was helping her daughter, say: 'I have never seen my daughter have such a good round. She looks like she is thinking for a change'. I frequently see dramatic improvements in performance when riders simply adopt a positive attitude and plan for their performance.

Negative thinking zaps one's energy and motivation: positive thinking energizes. When riders are not feeling motivated, I ask them to look at what they are thinking about. They often say that they are thinking about something negative, like being tired, feeling afraid, or trying to avoid something. Such emotions cause riders to become upset because the negative thoughts actually distract them from what they really want to do for themselves. With lots of enthusiasm, I remind such riders of their goal, of how far they have come, and ask them to re-focus their attention on thoughts which are challenging and exciting, and lead them down the path to the goal.

I also help them to find plans for coping with possible problems that they are predicting and allowing to interfere with their ability to take action. Riders often become nervous or afraid when they do not have a plan to cope with a possible problem. When you find yourself focusing more on a distraction, problem or fear, recognize that it is time to turn those thoughts around. Replace them with positive plans for overcoming the problem. This brings back the passion. Even if the fears do not go away immediately, continue to replace them with your positive coping plans and the positive will win through. This is mental toughness! Treat negative thoughts as a harmless nuisance, and take action.

Exercise: Negative and Positive Thinking

List three examples of when negative thinking hindered your performance.

1.

2.

3.

List three examples of when positive thinking was beneficial to you.

1.

2.

3.

Your attitude toward riding has developed from your beliefs about yourself as a rider. Complete the following checklist by circling the number that you think best represents your attitude toward yourself as a rider. You may want to do it twice; once for your attitude toward yourself as a rider, and once for your attitude toward yourself as a competitive rider.

The items across the top of the list represent positive beliefs about yourself. These positive beliefs support your positive attitude. The items across the bottom of the list represent negative beliefs about yourself. Any items that you circle with a value of four or less represent areas where you can work on developing positive beliefs about yourself. This work will enhance your attitude. Work on your attitude so that you can score all tens!

	Positive	Confident	Concentrated	Calm	Strong	Goals	Balanced
10	•	•	•	•	•	•	•
9	•	•	•	•	•	•	•
8	•	•	•	•	•	•	•
7	•	•	•	•	•	•	•
6	•	•	•	•	•	•	•
5	•	•	•	•	•	•	•
4	•	•	•	•	•	•	•
3	•	•	•	•	•	•	•
2	•	•	•	•	•	•	•
1	•	•	•	•	•	•	•
	Negative	Doubtful	Distracted	Nervous	Weak	No Goals	Emotional

Exercise: Accentuating the Positive

My positive beliefs about myself as a rider/competitor are:

My negative beliefs about myself as a rider/competitor are:

Write out a statement for each negative belief that turns it into a positive one. For example, a negative belief: 'Sometimes I choke in competition' can be turned into: 'I am an effective, relaxed competitor'.

Passion statement: The more you think about what you want to achieve, in a positive way, the more passion you develop. Write a statement that reminds you to focus on your passion and enjoy feeling the positive emotions. Sketch out where you are now, then sketch out where you want to be. *Start behaving as if you are where you want to be.*

'TUNING OUT' THE NEGATIVE

While learning to train your mind to tune out the doubts, it may be helpful to vizualize disconnecting, or pulling the plug on negative, doubting thoughts. You might also try learning to 'change the channel', as with the television, when you do not like what you are watching. Also, when competing, try only to watch the good competitors. When reviewing videotapes, watch poor performance only once, but watch the good tapes over and over.

In difficult situations, truly great riders are able to use a positive attitude to cope with the situation and find a solution.

Questionnaire: Attitude in Adversity

1. What is your attitude like when everything is going your way?

2. What is your attitude like when you experience difficulty or obstacles to your goals?

3. What differences can you see between the two attitudes?

When things are not going your way and your attitude is suffering, remind yourself to change the channel to the attitude that you have when things *are* going your way. List three ways that you will remind yourself to do this.

1.

2.

3.

Exercises: Developing Positive Belief

1. Make a commitment to believe in yourself, your goals, and your ability no matter what type of adversity you encounter. Develop the belief that you are stronger than your fears.

   Sample Affirmation: I am stronger than my fears and am able to work out any difficult situation that I may encounter with my positive belief in myself.

   Your Affirmation:

2. In times of adversity, force yourself to focus on successfully attaining your goal. Do this by writing a letter to yourself, a short essay about attaining your goal and how your attitude will allow you to do so, or use the mastery and coping exercises presented in Chapter 8.

   Sample Affirmation: I am able to visualize my goal in times of adversity.

   Your Affirmation:

3. When you encounter adversity or negative thinking, make a commitment to examine the negative thoughts and turn them into positive challenges.

The negative thoughts that I am experiencing are:

(a)

(b)

(c)

The challenge(s) in overcoming this situation is/are:

(a)

(b)

(c)

Write out an affirmation for each challenge. For example:

Negative belief: I cannot get on the right lead all the time.

Challenge: To pay attention to balance, positioning, and my aids.

Affirmation: I am able to check the balance, positioning of my horse, and my aids, prior to asking him to canter.

Practise releasing negative thoughts and focusing on the positive every day!

Developing a positive belief in yourself as a rider also involves learning to use the technique of 'possibility thinking'. Possibility thinking excludes limitations. Become a possibility thinker and list future possibilities that you want to attract for your riding career.

Practise your affirmations as you would practise riding – as much as possible.

OPENNESS TO CHANGE

Openness to change and innovation is another key to growth and success. This is achieved by challenging and testing traditional attitudes and beliefs in order to determine their validity and/or to find a more effective method. Innovation can only occur when riders are open to growth, believing that they can find a way to succeed.

5

Self-confidence: Without a Doubt

Self-confidence is effective thinking without doubts. It is especially important for riders because it is communicated to the horse – and horses often perform in accordance with the self-confidence of their riders. Self-confidence is a very personal matter. Developing and maintaining it involves getting into an honest, positive, approving relationship with yourself, in which you believe in yourself and your abilities. Only you can do this: no one else can do it for you. The benefits culminate in feelings of freedom.

Honesty is the first chapter of the book of wisdom. – Thomas Jefferson

For a moment, think about what goes into developing a good relationship with another person. You will probably come up with trust and honesty. The people with whom we tend to feel most comfortable are those we can trust, be honest with; from whom we do not have to hide our true selves. They are those people who believe in our abilities and approve of us regardless of our performance; those people who want the best for us and help us take good care of ourselves.

These are the key components to developing self-confidence. The ability to be honest with yourself leads you to feel good about yourself and self-confident because you are not hiding anything from yourself or being too self-critical. You thus become free from the tension that develops if you are trying to hide from yourself, or being too self-critical. Being honest with others stems from this (and further enhances self-confidence) because you do not feel the need to hide, or fear disapproval, or feel guilty or bad about yourself for not being honest.

WINNING DOES NOT CAUSE CONFIDENCE

You may think that when you win you will become self-confident, but it does not always work that way. One successful rider with whom I worked came to me because, while she won everything she could possibly win, she thought that she had very little self-confidence. At our first meeting she stated that she was not a very good rider and that she only won because her father bought her horses who were better than the competition. I pointed out to this 'good' rider that, while it is true that she has nice horses, she must have some ability to ride strong, good jumpers to so many consistent wins and high-score awards. For a while she did not want to acknowledge that she contributed to the wins. However, after discussing this issue, she slowly began to admit that she was a part of the winning formula; that she did ride well, and she recognized the self-confidence that was there.

SELF-TALK AND SELF-CONFIDENCE

It is important to develop your self-confidence while you are developing your riding skills. One way of doing this is by using positive self-talk. Your self-talk is your own way of communicating with yourself, which is why it is so important to develop self-talk that is honest, accurate and positive. As Dr. Robert Rotella, an internationally known sport psychologist suggests, tell yourself what you would tell your best friend. Far more frequently we tell our best friend positive things and tell ourself critical things, messages that create doubt. In a golf tape, Rotella cites an example of the tendency for golfers to be confident in others' abilities when the others are in tough situations, but to be self-critical in similar situations. Communicate positively to yourself, through your self-talk, during those moments of doubt and you will be on the road to building self-confidence. Learn to bet positively on yourself; bet that you can get out of difficult situations.

TAKING CARE OF YOURSELF

Learning to take good care of yourself also enhances self-confidence. By taking good care of your mental and physical health, diet and appearance you are letting yourself know that you are important and worthwhile. Often, riders take excellent care of their horses because they are so important to them, but forget to take good care of themselves. Learning to care for yourself as you would for your horse will cause you to feel more self-confident. The saying goes: 'Do unto others as you would have them do unto you', but you can also include 'Do unto yourself as you would do unto others'.

Lou Holtz, the highly successful football coach at the University of Notre Dame, says there are three questions that players often ask of coaches:

1. Can I trust you?
2. Do you believe in me?
3. Do you care about me?

You can ask these same questions of yourself with regard to self-confidence.

Self-confidence and determination are qualities that have enabled Michelle Ingold to become one of the best amateur competitors in the USA in a short period of time. In the spring of 1998, she was the High Point Amateur at the Essex CCI**.

Exercise: reasons for self-confidence

List three reasons why you can trust yourself as a rider.

1.

2.

3.

List three reasons why you can believe in your riding ability.

1.

2.

3.

List three reasons why it is important to care about yourself.

1.

2.

3.

TAKING CONTROL

When riders feel helpless, trapped, or out of control their self-confidence is low. Taking control of yourself, and responsibility for your actions, enhances self-confidence. This is the time to take your power back – focus on what you *want* to happen and take action. Act on procrastination. Make goals, decisions, and choices for *you* (no one else) and take action toward their realization. You will then notice that feelings of self-confidence emerge from your action. List daily steps that you can take to build confidence, take action and meditate on them.

As mentioned in other sections of the book, the ability to feel positive about yourself, regardless of your performance, enhances self-confidence. Think more about your successes; learn quickly from your mistakes and go forward. When the self-critic speaks, do not listen. The self-critic, the doubter, only causes you to get in your own way and upset yourself. Think of the self-critic as a pair of riding boots or a riding helmet that is much too big. It makes you trip all over the place or prevents clear vision. When the believer speaks, open your eyes, take it to heart and believe in yourself.

WHY SOME RIDERS ARE AFRAID OF SELF-CONFIDENCE

For some people, especially women, self-confidence has not historically been a characteristic that was socially acceptable in nice people. Often, cockiness and arrogance are confused with self-confidence. Self-confidence is feeling good about yourself and feeling that you can do something effectively. There is nothing wrong with feeling competent and successful. There is nothing wrong with trusting yourself. However, if you take it further than that and feel that you must let everyone outside the ring know how great you are, then that is not self-confidence, that is cockiness and arrogance.

When you enhance your self-confidence, other people may have a difficult time understanding you. They may have been comfortable with the old, self-critical you. They may now perceive you as a threat because of your self-confidence, and want you to go back to your old ways. At this point it is important to talk to those who are close to you about self-confidence; if they are your true friends, and truly supportive of you, they will understand that it is important for you to feel good about yourself. If they do not understand and like the self-critical you better, then you may want to re-think your relationship with them. It is a human tendency to want to keep others in their place; when you make changes often others around you undergo some kind of change also. When your energy changes it affects the energy of others, either in a negative or positive fashion.

TRAINING AND TRUSTING – CONFIDENCE IN COMPETITION

Dr. Robert Rotella, my adviser at the University of Virginia and a world-renowned sport psychologist, suggests that he would rather see an athlete not train a lot and really trust his or her ability and skill in competition, than see an athlete train really hard and then not trust any of it in competition. Whether you are ready or not, you must really trust yourself and believe that you can 'do it' in competition. This means going into the ring focused on what you want to happen, leaving the doubts somewhere else. That is strong confidence: it is *believing* you can, not wondering *whether* you can. That is the message I really focused on when returning to competition. While I was prepared, I trusted all my prior experiences and focused my mind on riding the courses as I had in the past. I did not focus on the fact that I had not competed for several years. Even if it is your first time in competition, believe you can do it like all the others and focus on performing in competition just as you have performed in training.

Transitions, such as changing your level of competition, riding a new horse, competing with a new horse, or changing trainers, can have an affect on your confidence. Your confidence level needs to make the same upward change as your skill level. To do this successfully, practise visualizing yourself riding effectively at the new level, on the new horse, or with the new trainer. Practise, practise, practise until you are comfortable and feeling confident.

SELF-SABOTAGE

Self-sabotaging thoughts are often a reflection of riders' attitudes, beliefs, or values regarding themselves, the horse, or the competitive situation. These thoughts programme the mind incorrectly and cause physical, as well as emotional reactions, which are often seen as performance blocks.

Mary, an FEI-level professional dressage rider, began experiencing peak performance in both practice and competition after learning to let go of the belief that her horses 'should' always go perfectly because she is a professional. When Mary's horses resisted her aids, she would become angry, thinking immediately when she felt the resistance that she was a very poor rider. Mary's perception caused

31

anger and was sabotaging her performance. When she learned to focus her attention on the present and on correcting the problem, rather than sabotaging herself with an irrational belief when things went wrong, improvement was dramatic.

Common Self-sabotaging Thoughts

1. I can't repeat a great performance

The art of performing consistently involves learning to cope with both the lows and highs. Sometimes, the latter can prove as difficult as the former, and some riders develop the sabotaging belief that they cannot repeat a great performance. This may come from a style of thinking that buys into the idea that people are only given one chance for success. The key to overcoming this is to keep winning and performing in perspective. Realize that you do not know how long your peak performance will last, enjoy it, ride each time in the present, and let go of past performances. By staying focused in the present you do not have to worry about trying to repeat the great performance (as a matter of fact *forget it*: put it out of your mind!) because you will be accepting that it is in the past.

This particular belief is often evident when riders, whose ultimate goals require the accumulation of points, become anxious or nervous. Much of their nervousness or anxiety comes because they are focusing on 'point chasing', and are consciously trying too hard or rigidly demanding a high-level performance of themselves so that they can win the ultimate award. Sometimes, this form of self-sabotage comes from doubting that the goal can be achieved, and worrying about that belief. When viewed realistically, however, all one can do is try to put in one's best effort each day, and believe that at the end of the year, it will have been good enough. *Fearing that you will not achieve your goal only interferes with concentration, destroys confidence, and creates self-sabotage. You disempower yourself when you focus on the importance of one event or one award.*

2. *Excuses prior to performance*

Making excuses for your performance *before* you perform is another way of sabotaging yourself. You may decide that it is all right if you do not ride well today because it is hot; the ground is bad; or your spouse was grouchy this morning. This type of sabotage works because you are focusing on what you expect to happen – not riding well. Why ride with this negative focus? Because it makes you feel safer; you do not have to put yourself and your confidence on the line since you have an excuse. However, although self-sabotage cushions failure, it inhibits peak performance: it is not a winning attitude.

3. *The 'let down'*

Riders often feel uncomfortable after a big win or great performance. This may occur after winning their first major competition, becoming champion at a prestigious show, winning at a new level, or simply at the end of an event or show that they had looked forward to for a long time. The discomfort that they are experiencing is a 'let down'. This is a natural occurrence, best handled by not dwelling too long on the 'big win', by resting, staying in the present, and being willing to move on. Doing well may cause you to feel guilty if you think that you do not deserve to win. This belief can sabotage future performance. When you win, you deserve it! Go ahead and enjoy it!

DOS AND DON'TS FOR DEVELOPING SELF-CONFIDENCE

As proposed by Craig Fischer, Ithaca College

DO:
- Acknowledge your defeats, and then dismiss them.
- Answer all compliments with 'Thank you'.

- Constantly be aware of and affirm your positive self-concept and goals. Create an environment of personal support.
- Actively pursue your goals; commit yourself to them.
- Share your goals only with those whom you trust.
- Support friends who ride in their endeavours – especially when they need it the most.
- Model yourself after someone successful, especially one who succeeded through hard work.
- View negative and destructive criticism as a direct statement of the critic's characteristics, not of who you are.
- Be a dreamer and dream great successes; harness the unlimited power of your imagination to reach your goals.
- Constantly acknowledge the fact that the only person you have control of is yourself.

DON'T
- Apologize to others when you make a mistake or ride poorly; this simply doubles the negative impact and serves no useful purpose.
- Allow negative internal dialogue to be your major self-coaching strategy.
- Criticize others in an unthinking or destructive manner; always leave room for them to perceive something positive.
- Attach your thoughts and feelings about yourself exclusively to your victories or defeats.
- Compare your performance with everyone else's.
- Constantly excuse your performance.
- Depend on others for affirmation and support.
- Minimize or make light of your successes.
- Feel awkward or be embarrassed about giving positive reinforcement to friends.
- Disregard a friend's or coach's encouragement.
- Dwell on mistakes.

Questionnaire: Analysing and Evaluating Self-confidence

1. Do you tend to use your accomplishments/successes as a measure of your self-worth?

2. After experiencing a setback or failure when riding, do you let that interfere with the rest of your life, your training, and positive thoughts regarding your self-worth?

3. Do you have a high level of confidence when training and lose it when in competition?

4. List ways by which you can transfer the confidence that you have when training to competitive situations.

5. Do you rely on comments from other people to give you self-confidence, or do you rely on your own thoughts regarding your self-worth?

6. Do you let people walk all over you?

7. Are you able to approve of yourself when you are not receiving approval from other people?

8. List ways that you can approve of yourself no matter what is happening around you.

9. What is your perception of your confidence level? How do you think others perceive your confidence level?

9. Make a time line of your riding career (see below).

1st ride   Present

Time Line

Note the changes in level that you have made. What was your self-confidence like when you were first starting? Has it changed as you have developed as a rider? I have found that often ability level changes but self-confidence does not. For example, a rider may be competing over significant jumping courses with the self-confidence and/or self-image of a beginner. If your self-confidence/self-image has been left behind, write an affirmation that brings it into the present, and meditate on it daily
Sample affirmation: I am a confident showjumping rider. Or, I am a confident professional rider.

6

Motivation

What moves you to action? Before reading this chapter, answer the following questions. Answer each question as completely as you can.

1. How much motivation is necessary for you to put in a good performance?

2. Rate your motivation to practise; to compete.

3. Do you need more motivation for 'big' competitions or performances?

4. Do you believe that someday you will be able to ride perfectly?

THE PERFECTIONIST RIDER

Odd though it may seem, perfectionism can inhibit action. The following case studies show how this happens – it may be that you can relate to some of these riders' attitudes.

Karen

Karen was, for many years, a successful competitor. She was confident and excited when she first entered the arena of international competition, and she performed really well at her first show. At the second show, she found herself looking for reasons why she did not belong at that level. Karen believed that the judges' scores were indicative of whether or not she should remain in competition. If she received high scores, she thought that she belonged. If she received low scores, she became very upset and thought it was time to quit riding. Since there was variation in her performance and in the judges' scores, she never quite knew if she was or was not 'worthy', or deserving of international competition. She focused her attention so hard on these beliefs that she neglected to pay attention to the process, to the technical aspects of riding, while in competition. She recalls her experience thus:

> I became very self-critical, constantly comparing my performance to that of others and looking for any reason I could find that would tell me that I did not belong in international competition. I found myself constantly looking for criticism from the other competitors that would support my belief. If my horse was the least bit less than perfect, I would immediately think I was a bad rider and he would immediately react with resistance. I would become more frustrated, fight with him, and get off feeling defeated. I would feel that way for several days, sometimes weeks. Next I found a trainer who supported my negative belief in myself. That trainer broke me down to where I thought I did not know how to ride and felt like I needed a year off, and he also broke my horse down.

'When my mind is focused on perfection, mistakes are all that I can see', said Karen. Karen's self-talk often involved a dialogue similar to this: 'I do not want to make any mistakes, I do not want to appear as if I am not a professional rider'. 'If I make a mistake or have a poor performance, it means I am not a professional, at least to me.' Karen thus talked herself into making mistakes and riding poorly.

Laura

Laura, an intermediate-level adult amateur rider, had a dream that often turned into a nightmare in reality. Her goal was to perform well at a horse show. She had tried several times at various shows over the years, and with several different trainers and horses. The result was always the same. She would leave the show frustrated and disappointed. Sometimes she would not even make it into the show ring because she and her horse were so nervous.

After the heartbreak of each show had dissipated, Laura would try again, with high hopes and dreams of being able to ride in a show the way that she could at home. Laura could not figure out what the problem was. She had a very nice, well-schooled horse who was attractive, a good mover, and a good jumper. Both horse and rider had exquisite show gear and were groomed as if they were going to the National Horse Show. Laura never missed a practice session, took plenty of lessons from trainers with excellent reputations, and wanted to do well, but never did.

You train hard, set high standards, and make sure your horse is well turned out and athletically fit, but are you really training for success and peak performance? All riders want to ride well and shine, but sometimes training for success is actually training for perfection, which often leads to disappointment and failure when perfectionist tendencies become unmanageable. You may be unknowingly setting yourself up for anxiety rather than success and enjoyment of the sport. Everyone has experienced pre-competition jitters at one time or another, but if you repeatedly experience nervousness that you cannot use to your advantage, the kind that makes you feel paralysed, you may need to look at your thoughts, attitudes, and beliefs regarding the importance of perfection and competition.

Mary

'I want to win more than anything else this season', said Mary, a showjumping rider. 'But even more that that, I must perform perfectly.' Mary was so focused on 'being perfect' at a show that she forgot how to ride.

Results and perfection can become such important performance factors to perfectionist riders that they spend most of their mental energy worrying about how terrible it would be if they did not do well, or made even a small error. Believing that results can be controlled, demanding perfection, fearing mistakes, all add up to a rider who becomes nervous and rigid in competition. Karen found it hard to work out a problem in competition because, if she did not get it right the very second that she tried, she would become angry, frustrated and highly critical of her riding ability – and her horse displayed those emotions too!

The positive side of perfectionism is that it does motivate riders to train: it helps them to set goals and to work daily toward those goals. However, even in this context, it can act as a two-edged sword. 'Perfectionism will get a rider two-thirds of the way to the top, but can become a block to peak performance at that point', says Dr. Robert Rotella. Perfectionism sounds positive, evoking images of winners, those who are attentive to details and want to do a job right the first time around. That is fine when it comes to the early stages of training, but when the motor patterns are established and skills are well learned, usually when the rider is two-thirds of the way to the top, it is necessary to back off from the perfectionist tendencies because they begin to become a hindrance to performance rather than an enhancement. Some margin for error is necessary. Criticism, questioning, and punishment for mistakes destroy self-confidence, a rider's ability to trust their horse, their decision-making ability, and their skills. It only teaches blame, shame, and guilt – emotions that riders use to put more pressure on themselves and feel bad about themselves. Basically, they are unable to ride instinctively and get into the flow of their performance, which is what it takes to ride really well. Kathy Newman, rider and trainer of the 1994 AHSA Working Horse of the Year, Ashford Castle, believes that the 'three most important ingredients to great riding are instinct, trust, and feel'. Perfectionism, based in unrealistic beliefs, often teaches riders to not trust their instincts.

Letting go of perfectionism and coping successfully with challenges enabled Kathy Doyle Newman to produce *Ashford Castle*, one of the most successful show hunters ever. Still showing at the age of 16, *Ashford Castle* has probably won more hunter championships than any other horse in American history.

Beating the Perfectionist 'Block'

Robert Rotella suggests that 'it is more important for riders to have a great attitude in response to their mistakes than it is to think that they are never supposed to make mistakes – that quality separates good riders from great riders'. That great attitude includes accepting that mistakes are just as much a part of riding as doing things well. The mistakes do not have to be judged as good or bad, they just need to be corrected. Perfectionist riders tend to become emotional about mistakes; they will benefit from learning to accept their mistakes and move on. Mistakes happen to all riders – even the greatest of the great make mistakes. When teaching, it is important to make careful use of positive reinforcement and feedback so as not to create perfectionism in students. Refraining from making comments on a rider's mistakes is an effective way to emphasize the positive, build confidence, and eliminate the negative. This method focuses the rider's attention on what they want to happen, rather than on what they do not want to happen (the mistake). By shifting the rider's attention from what was wrong with the performance to what was right with it, the rider's feelings of competence and confidence are strengthened. This approach eases the pressure that riders often feel when they try to ride perfectly, especially in competition. 'The perfectionist rider, who is already too self-critical, does not need any more support for his/her self-criticism', suggests Rotella. So far as percentages go, I estimate that 90 per cent of the riders with whom I work in my classes and private practice are perfectionists.

Once a rider comes to grips with how perfectionism is affecting them, their performance usually surges forward. They forget about what can go wrong and feel more relaxed; they are able to focus their mind on the appropriate technical aspects, they get their 'eye' and 'feel' back, and they are able to cope more effectively with unexpected situations or distractions which they may encounter during their ride.

For Karen, coming to grips with perfectionism meant 'dubbing' a new mental tape loop for her head, one that focused on what she *could* do and allowed her to ignore mistakes, rather than blaming herself or feeling guilty for not being perfect:

> Now, as I work daily on training my mind for peak performance, I have developed a personal philosophy that includes thinking in ways that enhance my performance and I look for reasons to believe in myself and my horses. When I find myself becoming self-critical, I take a 'time-out' and re-focus my thoughts on what I have done right. I think of myself as a professional who is able to compete on the international level, whereas before I thought of myself as an imposter.

Even mistake-free performances can throw perfectionist riders off balance! From such performances, perfectionists often create such high expectations for the future that they become stressed out. They think that the performance may have been a fluke, but they have a compulsion to repeat it and feel that, since it may have been a fluke, they have no control over whether or not they can do so. Julie, who rides in the Amateur-Owner Hunter division, frequently felt frozen after a good ride, thinking that there was no way she could repeat her performance, let alone improve upon it. She then adopted the philosophy that each ride is separate and unique; that, in order to ride in the flow, she must focus her attention in the present. She learned that expectations and thoughts about future performance only distracted her from focusing in the present. She stopped counting points and wins, and concentrated instead on riding in the here and now, accepting each performance as it happened. She realized that focusing her attention on each stride and jump was what kept her trusting and riding in an instinctive manner. She now understood that trying to predict future performances and control them had been a waste of time that only distracted her focus of attention.

ARE YOU A PERFECTIONIST?

If so, you probably related to certain aspects of the earlier case studies. To find out more about your attitudes, answer the following questions.

1. Do you base your self-esteem on your results? Do you only feel good about yourself when you are riding well? After riding poorly are you able to 'let go' of the performance, or does it cause you to feel bad until the next time you perform well?

2. Do you become irrational or emotional when things are not going your way, or in reaction to your mistakes?

3. Do you emphasize your mistakes and weaknesses and point them out to others, whilst neglecting to give equal weight to your strengths and accomplishments?

4. Do you believe your way is the only way?

5. Do you think vacations are a waste of time and money?

6. Are you over-critical of yourself and others?

7. Do you find yourself constantly 'what-iffing', and controlling, which creates self-doubt and fear?

8. Have you ever had a performance that was 'good enough' in your own mind?

9. When riding, are you able to concentrate on the present moment or are most of your thoughts about the future, about evaluation of your performance, or just worrisome?

10. Do you ride better in practice than in competition? Explain the way you feel the two differ.

11. Do you feel that practice is unnecessary to good performance?

12. Do you feel as if nothing is ever good enough?

13. Do you feel that there is not enough good to go around, or that you only get one chance at success?

14. Do you ever think that if you have too good a time, or are too successful, something bad will happen, or it will be taken away?

OVERCOMING PERFECTIONISM

Here are some tips for overcoming the negative aspects of perfectionism.

1. Learn to accept mistakes; imperfection and failure as just as much parts of riding as performing well.

2. In response to your mistakes, learn from them and move forward. Dwelling on the mistake increases the probability that you will continue to make the same mistake over and over again.

3. Work toward finding solutions to problems rather than trying to avoid the problem.

4. View problems and challenges, and react to them, in a non-evaluative, confident manner rather than an emotional manner.

5. Look for several ways to solve a problem or correct a mistake.

6. Take time off when you need it – when you are physically tired or mentally/emotionally drained.

7. Look for the good in yourself and others.

8. Focus your attention in the present and accept what is happening in the present.

9. Accept yourself as a worthwhile human being regardless of your performance.

Also, try the following exercises.

Exercise: Substituting Perfectionist Beliefs

First, list any perfectionist beliefs that you hold, then write a statement in which you explain to yourself how each belief hurts you rather than helps you. Then, formulate a new belief that will replace the old belief.

Having done so, visualize throwing the old belief away, or disconnecting your mind from it, and meditate on your new belief. You may want to work on only one belief at a time, perhaps for a week each. Remember, you want to remain 'perfection-free' while doing this work!

Exercise: Managing Self-criticism

List three ways by which you will manage your desire to be over-analytical, self-critical, or over-evaluative of your performance. Then, list the ways in which you will benefit from managing these tendencies.

Finally, produce a personal affirmation based on the example below.

Sample Affirmation: My riding is improving because I have let go of the perfectionist tendencies that interfere with my motivation and performance.

Perfectionism and Concentration
Perfectionists tend to focus on the future or on living in the past.

Breaks in their concentration are caused by worrisome thoughts about the future or past; performance results; their need to achieve more; their needs for perfection; and their ability to paralyse themselves by being too analytical.

Thoughts that contain many 'shoulds' and 'oughts' are characteristic of perfectionists. The fallacy in this style of thinking is that if an individual 'should have done; or 'ought to do' something it means that they cannot accept what they actually did in the past, or that what they want to do now is the right thing. Such thinking causes guilt and shame. It is difficult to be self-accepting when one's self-talk contains many 'shoulds' and 'oughts'. By eliminating these pressure-filled thoughts riders can become accepting of themselves. Attention will be focused on the reality of the present and future rather than on condemnation of the self and of past performance.

Monitor your self-talk for 'shoulds' and 'oughts'. When you hear them, replace the thoughts with ones that are accepting of your performance. In order to live in the present, you must disconnect from the past or from worry about the future.

Affirmation: I am living life, moment by moment, in the present. I pay attention to what is going on around me in each moment.

Learning the Balancing Act
In order to think realistically, it is helpful for perfectionists to recognize and appreciate their talents, abilities, and shortcomings. Often they fight, struggle against, or deny the existence of shortcomings; this makes it impossible for them to improve upon their shortcomings. Perfectionists can learn to recognize and accept the fact that being human is being imperfect.

Exercise: Balancing Strengths and Weaknesses

1. Make a list headed 'My strengths as a rider.'

2. Make a list headed 'My weaknesses as a rider.'

3. I criticize myself for my weaknesses when I say to myself:
(a)

(b)

(c)

4. From now on, I commit to becoming non-evaluative about my weaknesses.

Affirmation: I will frequently remind myself of my strengths, such as ...., and will accept my weaknesses and work toward making them my strengths.

5. I can bring the joy back to my riding by:
(a)

(b)

(c)

Patience, Humour and Rest

Patience

Patience is a vital ingredient to overcoming perfectionism. Improvements do not come overnight, especially in high-level performers. Often, the closer one is to the goal, the greater the patience needed because the improvements occur in smaller increments. When improvements do occur it is necessary for perfectionists to recognize them and reward themselves for being patient. The following anonymous quotation can be turned into an affirmation: 'Time is nature's way of keeping everything from happening at once'.

Humour

It will never hurt perfectionists to add some humour to their daily lives. Since perfectionists tend to take themselves too seriously, humour can teach them about the lighter side of life.

Exercise: Humour

List three ways that you can add humour to your daily life

1.

2.

3.

Rest

Since perfectionists tend to over-train, it is very difficult for them to take vacations. They often feel that they will get too far behind, which causes them to become fearful of taking time off. The perfectionist must learn to accept that rests and breaks can help performance as much, or more, than hard work because they help dissipate the fatigue that builds up from training.

Performance often improves rather than declines after a break.

'Letting go' – a Summary

There comes a point when every rider must back off from perfectionist tendencies and learn to trust, get into the flow, and ride in the present. Learning to let go of the results, learning not to try so hard, and learning to relax and trust themselves will allow even perfectionist riders to perform at their peak.

Here is a list of tips to assist perfectionist riders to achieve this:

- Keep winning and losing in perspective.
- Learn to be self-accepting of your talents and abilities as well as your weaknesses.
- Let go of guilt and self-criticism.
- Deal with the negative emotions as they occur rather than trying to avoid or deny those emotions.
- Enjoy riding and have fun with the process at all levels.
- Add humour to each day.

UNDERACHIEVING RIDERS

Underachieving riders are often very talented performers. Coner, a rising star in the showjumping arena, always seems to rise to the level of competition, even though he lacks the motivation to practise. He performs well under pressure, yet when the pressure is off, he has trouble motivating himself to practise and condition his horse. He feels that practising is a waste of time, and his belief is often reinforced when he wins at shows for which he has practised very little beforehand.

Like Coner, many people have the ability to get into the flow of their performance but, often, they seem to lack the ability to realize their full potential. Their lack of motivation is usually evidenced by their poor practice habits and lack of goals. They are often labelled lazy, and frustrate their parents, coaches, and teachers. These riders usually have not developed the type of work ethic that perfectionists have. They do not see the relationship between hard work and success. It is often the case with such riders that they achieved a lot of success at an early age through their natural talent, without having to work hard. Skill development was a natural, easy process.

The 'lazy' attitude that is often characteristic of under-motivated riders is learned from lack of challenge. When under-motivated riders are faced with a higher level of competition and with competitors of equal or greater ability than themselves they often feel frustrated and under-prepared. They make excuses for their performance, and feel helpless with regard to improving it. When faced with challenging competitors, under-motivated riders often fail, become frustrated and then quit, instead of learning how to set goals and practise in order to bring their performance up to that of their competitors.

Concentration Focus of Under-motivated Riders
Under-motivated riders tend to live in the present, which allows them to focus their attention, when performing, in the present. While this is the appropriate time-frame for competition, an overall lack of thought about the future and results makes setting goals, preparation and practice difficult.

These riders also tend to have a great memory for their successes but easily forget their mistakes. They have the ability to treat mistakes as accidents, and do not spend time worrying about them. Some view practice as an opportunity to make more mistakes, which reinforces their belief that practice is not important to performance. *Sometimes, also, their fear of failure prevents them from practising: if they do not have goals, then they cannot fail.* But what under-motivated riders need to learn is that if they try and fail, they will be further along the process, and better riders, than if they just quit. They can also learn *to enjoy the process*, which will bring them feelings of self-satisfaction. Finally, they need to know that they do not have to share their goals with anyone – which allows them to avoid feelings of embarrassment or criticism from others if they do not accomplish them.

Increasing Motivation in Under-motivated Riders
Under-motivated riders should be encouraged to:
- Learn to enjoy practice and learn to recognize the value of practising.
- Set realistic goals that emphasize the process as well as the product (see Chapter 7).
- Reward their own practice with something meaningful to themselves.
- Create practice sessions which have their own intrinsic rewards.
- Compete against riders whose ability is equal to or better than their own.

When working with young riders who are very talented it is useful to ensure that they are provided with opportunities to compete against others with similar talents, so that success will not be too easy. Doing this at an early age may forestall later frustration when these riders are competing against others with equal or greater ability, and need to practise but don't know how to do so effectively.

WHEN MOTIVATION IS BALANCED

The theory of learned effectiveness (Rotella and Coop 1985) states that there is a 'way to perceive and react to the world of sport that will maximize your performance in it'. Here are some hints for developing a balanced perspective.

1. View problems as positive challenges rather than as stressors, and attract positive means to solve them.
2. Seek out people who are positive and supportive of you, and events which have similar effects.
3. Try to avoid entrapment in self-pity, jealousy, hatred, envy, and negative people.
4. Accept the fact that failure is part of competition and learn to move on quickly from failure.
5. Believe in yourself and realize that you are a worthy human being – win, lose, or draw. That is, try to maintain high self-esteem regardless of your performance.
6. Assess your feelings, attitudes, and beliefs as well as your physical condition. When it is necessary, take time off or work harder, and do so without feeling guilt or remorse.
7. Realize that the world is not always fair and accept that fact.
8. Free your mind from thoughts that involve 'shoulds', 'oughts', 'musts', and 'demands'.
9. Do not let others (parents, peers, coaches, trainers) predict your success. Set your own goals and refuse to be pushed or limited by others' views on your ability.
10. Realize that there is a training mentality and a competitive mentality. When training, work on weaknesses to make them your strengths. When competing, focus on your strengths and trust them.

Exercise: Balancing Motivation

1. Which of the three motivation levels – perfectionist, under-achiever, learned effective – do you tend to fall into?

For perfectionists, list the pros and cons of this level. Do the pros justify the cons? List ways that you can convince yourself to let go of thinking about results; ways by which you can let go of your needs for achievement, approval, and perfection and list ways by which you can develop patience with your new attitude.

For underachievers, list ways by which you can increase your motivation. List fears that may presently be keeping you from setting goals and practising, and then list ways that you can work on overcoming those fears.

For 'learned effectives' (those who believe they have established a balance), list ways in which your attitude enhances your ability to train and perform. List ways that you will stay committed to your attitude during tough times, such as level changes, slumps, or drops in performance.

2. List five learned effective tendencies (from those shown on page 54) that you would like to learn.

(a)

(b)

(c)

(d)

(e)

3. List five ways that you will *use* these tendencies to help you maintain balance.

    (a)

    (b)

    (c)

    (d)

    (e)

4. Make use of visualization (see Chapter 8).

    For perfectionists, practice letting go of the thoughts and attitudes that are keeping you from letting go!

    For underachievers, visualize energizing yourself for practice. Visualize developing practice habits in which you have an effective level of energy. Practise motivating yourself when you do not feel like working.

7

Forget About the Outcome

At the last show of the season, Bill was neck and neck with another competitor for the State Horse of the Year award in his division. At that show he had two horses entered in the division, and it was on the better of the two that he was in contention for the award. He was very worried about his rival, who was just a few points behind him, and competing at that show. While Bill became champion in the division, he did so on the 'wrong' horse; the one who was not in contention for the award. On the horse who was in contention for the honours, he made a lot of mistakes. What happened essentially was that Bill had flawless rides on the horse that he did not care about. When on the better horse, all he could think about was winning on that horse, which caused him to become anxious and tense and make mistakes that he usually did not make. This rider learned the hard way that worrying about results had a direct effect on his performance.

After this show, we evaluated the mind game that he had engaged in. The next time Bill was under competitive pressure, he was able to relax and get into the flow of his performances. Bill worked very hard on learning to believe that riders are most in control when they let go of the results and trust the process.

Learning to 'leave the results to take care of themselves' and get into the flow are key concepts. The ability to do this allows riders to become involved in the process and the associated technical aspects, and frees the mind from the tension and confusion that are created from trying to control results – which are not controllable. Every time I tell riders that they do not have to try harder, or try to control the results, I hear a sigh of relief. Performing your best is not a painful endeavour. Remember, the goal is to ride in the flow; in the peak performance zone.

Conflicts develop in some competitors because equestrian sports, just like most other competitive sports, teach their participants to be result-oriented. Riders learn to value the importance of winning and sometimes lose sight of the *process* of performing well. High-point awards, rankings, placement in classes and events, and some competitions being billed as more important than others, all help to create the conflict. It is important to understand that *external rewards for competition do not have anything to do with actually performing the sport, or any involvement in the process of performance.* When riders' attention becomes concentrated on the externals of competition (awards, other competitors, 'big' classes or shows, judges) rather than the process of riding and performance, the results are usually anxiety, choking, and performance errors rather than peak performance.

The performance errors occur because riders are neglecting to pay attention to their riding, or trying too hard, or simply making a mistake. Anxiety and choking arise from trying to control the results, or from perfectionist attitudes. Results cannot be controlled, because it is impossible to control the performance of other competitors, the difficulty of the courses, or the preferences of the judges. When trying to control results, riders put so much pressure on themselves to perform perfectly that they end up choking.

Most of the time, trying too hard does not result in a flowing performance. Instead, it creates anxiety and tension, influences which render it impossible for riders to flow. Anxiety-ridden thoughts remind riders of all the possible disasters that might occur: this, in turn, creates mental confusion, physical tension, feelings of incompetence, and the inability to concentrate or focus on the task at hand.

Exercise: Determining the Controllable; Letting Go the Uncontrollable

1. Have you experienced situations where you became over-concerned with controlling results and/or tried to force your performance to happen, rather than let it happen?

2. If yes, list what you could control; what you could not.

3. Agree to let go of that which you cannot control.

FOCUS ON THE PROCESS

Misha is an amateur rider in her thirties. She had not competed for several years, and in the past had always ridden fully schooled horses. In the November when she came to me, she had just purchased a very expensive, slightly green horse to show in the Amateur Owner Hunter division. Misha's goals were to show the following winter on the Florida circuit, continue showing throughout the year, qualify for the indoor shows and, at the conclusion of the year, sell her horse for a profit. After stating her goals, Misha also told me that she was out of shape, frightened of jumping 3 ft 6 in, did not have a good 'eye', and basically had little self-confidence. She wanted me to help her put it all together by mid-January.

Since there were many obstacles to overcome in a short time, Misha committed to daily mental and physical training. We started out by making plans for getting her in better physical shape, looking at her fears regarding jumping 3 ft 6 in and teaching her to believe that she could successfully jump that height, and also assessing whether she had the right trainer. As it turned out, this rider had a very serious case of performance anxiety. Throughout our sessions we worked on those fears. When she was away at shows, we had phone conferences. Early on, it became apparent that her trainer had little confidence in her riding ability, so it was necessary for her to make a change. She found a nationally acclaimed trainer who not only had confidence in her riding ability but, in the first lesson, unsolicited, told her that she had a very nice 'eye'. One big problem was solved!

Throughout the Florida Circuit, Misha programmed her mind using mastery and coping tapes (see Chapter 8) that were developed for her, and also consulted with me frequently by phone. She honoured her commitment to the daily process and the results were somewhat amazing. Not only was she riding well around the 3 ft 6 in courses, she was actually winning classes. She earned enough points in Florida to qualify for the Devon Horse Show.

Midway through the show season, however, Misha and her husband became over-worried about points, wondering if she would have enough to qualify for the big autumn indoor shows. Her husband wanted her to abandon the process that had brought her good results and focus only on getting points. I urged her to stick with the process and trust that she would get the results. After consultation with both parties, her husband agreed to suspend his concern about points for one month. (I told my client that, after one month, she and her husband could think about points again.) Fortunately, by that time, points were a non-issue because she had earned enough to go to the Pennsylvania National Horse Show and the Washington International Horse Show. In fact, Misha missed qualifying for the National Horse Show by only a few points.

During the spring and summer she became more self-confident by working daily on reprogramming her mind. However, one of her biggest fears was riding in front of her former trainer. She had to overcome this, and much of our time was spent working on that issue. In September, her anxiety level rose again, with the approach of the indoor shows. We focused our sessions on coping with her anxiety by formulating coping strategies, and Misha also practised competing at the indoor shows by simulating indoor show conditions during training.

After successful performances at the indoor shows, and receiving the offer on the horse that she had hoped for, this rider had accomplished her goals. She had worked very hard mentally to overcome her anxieties and the numerous obstacles that stood between her and her goals. She followed her dream, focused on the process and worked through the obstacles. In this way she attained her dreams.

GOALS AND GOAL-SETTING

Without our work on mental preparation, Misha would have become a victim of her own doubts and fears. Instead, she attained a high level of success and received a valuable lesson in overcoming self-doubt by following her dream. In order to do this, Misha had set very specific goals. Goal-setting, a motivational technique, helps guide riders toward their dreams and provides helpful feedback along the way as to where they are in relation to their goals. Goals may be long-term, intermediate, and short-term, and it helps to distinguish between product and process goals. Product goals are measurable – for example, winning a class. Process goals are not so measurable –

they encompass such matters as becoming a stronger competitor, improving the consistency of performance, or improving confidence. They involve steps to which one must remain committed on a daily basis in order to achieve the product goals.

Detailed goal-setting is very effective for increasing motivation and maintaining the appropriate focus. Goals help to organize and sort out the necessary daily, weekly, monthly, and yearly tasks for the pursuit of excellence in riding. In underachieving riders, goal-setting is a necessity in order that they understand each step toward their goal. However, if a perfectionist athlete is highly obsessed with goals, then it may not be useful to spell out their goals specifically, since this fuels the perfectionism in them, and increases stress. For perfectionists, goals should be more process-oriented; focusing on relaxing, letting go, and overcoming negative attitudes and behaviours.

The most important aspect of goal-setting is that the goals are suitable for both horse and rider. Effective goals are:

- Achievable – which means within the reach of the rider's and horse's talents and abilities.
- Believable – riders must accept the goals as being possible.
- Conceivable – riders must really feel that they can accomplish their goals.
- Desirable – the goals are set and desired by the riders who are attempting them, not imposed by other people who want to gain from them.
- Flexible – which means that they can be modified or altered when necessary.
- Measurable – so that riders receive information with regard to where they are in relation to the achievement of their goals.

(Bunker, Rotella, and Reilly 1985)

Goal-setting Example 1

Date: January 1999

PRODUCT GOALS

Long-term
Selection as United States Equestrian Team Member for the winter shows.

Intermediate
1. Win three Grands Prix (trials) this year and place in all Grands Prix entered.
2. Win three Grands Prix next year and place in top five in all Grands Prix entered.
3. Reduce body fat to 20 per cent.

Short-term
Win one Grand Prix in this year. Place in top five in all Grands Prix this year.

PROCESS GOALS

Short-term (this year)
- Ride in Grands Prix in Florida.
- Work on speed and turns.
- Weight and aerobic training three days a week for 1½ hours. Bike and exercise workout. Walk three miles a day on other days. Stretch before riding.
- Daily visualization practice and monthly sport psychology session. Phone calls when necessary.
- Ride in Upperville, Ox Ridge, Devon, Lake Placid, Cleveland, Philadelphia and indoor Grands Prix, rotating three horses.

- Ride five horses per day, five to six days a week when at home.
- Flat lessons once a week.
- Schooling lessons with three to five former USET riders who have been to the Olympics.
- One 'mental health' day per week – play tennis, visit theatre, socialize, shop, read, etc.
- One week vacation after Florida and one in late summer.
- Watch old Olympic videos when frustrated or down on motivation.
- Keep a list of attitudes and thoughts to work on.

Intermediate

- Compete in Europe at five shows (winter/spring).
- Lessons from three European Olympians.
- Compete in qualifying Grands Prix June–December.
- Same physical and mental training as previous year and same scheduled vacations.

Long-term (two years from now)

- Winter – Compete on Florida Circuit. Continue lessons from former Olympians. Continue mental and physical training, diet, and vacations.
- Spring: Work on weaknesses from Florida. Ride in qualifiers. Keep everything in perspective. Emphasize mental health days to keep balance. Remember there is always another chance to do this and the work that I've done will get me there at some point in time.

Goal-setting Example 2

Date: January 1999

PRODUCT GOALS

Long-term
To become a knowledgeable and competent horse owner. Purchase a horse in June. Cost – $5,000.00.

Intermediate
Have $3,000.00 saved by August. Begin buying some of the equipment and start to look for a place to keep the horse.

Short-term
Start purchasing equipment.

PROCESS GOALS

Long-term
To enjoy riding and caring for own horse. Ride five times a week. Take a few lessons each month.

Intermediate
Be able to walk, trot, and canter and jump low fences (2 ft) by August.

Short-term
January – start taking riding lessons 2–3 times per week from a good instructor. Start reading books on horse care or attend horse management lectures. Learn about the costs of horse owning.

WITH GOALS COME OBSTACLES

I do not want to sound negative here, but this heading is a fact. Most books on goal-setting forget to tell their readers about obstacles. Thus many people set wonderful goals, which they never attain because they do not expect the obstacles, nor do they plan effective methods for overcoming them.

The obstacles to your goals can be handled in much the same manner as a jump. Sometimes you just jump right over; sometimes it is a struggle to get to the other side; sometimes it takes more than one try and more than one approach. This is where creativity, thinking positively with an open mind, persistence, and perseverance come in. Horses are excellent at teaching this lesson to their riders.

The way to overcome obstacles is to view them positively. They are present for a reason: they test your commitment to a goal. Obstacles ask whether you really want something: without the obstacles there is no challenge. After you have cleared the obstacles there are always more, new, challenging obstacles to be faced! 'Throw your heart over the fence and the horse will follow.'

Hints for Overcoming Obstacles
- Set goals for overcoming the challenge.
- Be patient; let time work for you.
- Look for creative solutions.
- If nothing is working, let go for a while and come back to the problem later.
- When an obstacle causes you to go off your path, develop the ability to get right back on. Focus on the goal, visualize yourself achieving it.
- Sometimes, just as with jumping, you need to lower the obstacle to get over it, and then put it back up.
- Learn to be flexible in your approach.

- Give yourself lots of time to practise overcoming challenging obstacles.
- Take action; frustration and helplessness results from non-action.

Overcoming Your Own Mental Objections

During the goal-setting process you may find that the voice inside your mind is presenting reasons why you cannot achieve your goals. While you are setting your goals it is important to listen to those thoughts and write them down. Using the Grand Prix rider's example, let's work through the negative thoughts.

1. 'I do not ride well enough to make the winter team.'
2. 'Other people might criticize my goal as being foolish.'
3. 'I do not deserve to be successful.'
4. 'If I set a goal this high, what if I fail?'
5. 'I'm almost there . . . it's not going to happen.'

The next step is to write out positive affirmations that dispute the validity of the negative thoughts.

1. 'I am a good rider and I have competed successfully against others who have been on the teams.'
2. 'What other people think is none of my business. My confidence in my goals is all that matters.'
3. 'I owe it to myself to find out how good I can be.'
4. 'If I fail I will be a better, more experienced rider than I am now.'
5. 'I'm there and enjoying it.'

Now, throw away the negative list and spend time daily meditating on your affirmations: **Each day at _ o'clock I will meditate.** Also, post your affirmations in a place where you will see them often.

Shakti Gawain, author of the best-selling book *Creative Visualization* suggests that you draw a picture of your goals, or make a collage with images of your goals and view them regularly.

AFTER THE DREAM

When riders get close to the achievement of a goal or dream – especially if they invested years of preparation – it is important to think about setting new goals. Often, riders feel disillusioned and let down after accomplishing a long-term goal. Having a new plan for the future helps ease the let-down, because it tells riders that there is a future for them. Without a plan, riders feel disoriented and lost. While the new goal might simply be to take time off and enjoy life, specific ways to accomplish that goal will help the transition.

8

Visualize What You Want to Happen

'For the first time, I feel like I can really ride my horse', exclaimed Susan, a three-day event rider, after participating with her horse in a sport psychology workshop. Susan had an experience in the clinic which proved that visualization is a key to successful performance. Late in the second mounted session, the group was working on executing a course that tested their ability to focus on changes in pace. Susan's first attempt, had it been scored, would have been in the 70s. Her second attempt, after the other riders went, was a disaster – a low 30s score. When asked what she was thinking prior to the second trip (we hoped that, at this point, she would have formulated a plan to execute the course a little more effectively), Susan said she was thinking about how late it was in the day, and how she was tired. I took her aside, asked her to visualize the course as I talked her through how to ride it, and then asked her to verbalize her plan to ride it, and visualize it again. Her third attempt was almost flawless – probably a score in the 90s. Everyone was amazed! This example proved, without doubt, that Susan's thoughts and mental preparation had a significant effect on her performance.

FOCUSING ON DISTRACTIONS

Prior to the first class at a major show, I asked Keri, a junior hunter rider with whom I had just begun to work, what she was thinking. Keri had appeared nervous whilst warming-up. She exclaimed that she was afraid that she was going to crash through all the jumps. Focused on fear, this negative visualization gave her no mental guidance regarding how to ride the course. We discussed her fear, which helped her to release it. Next, I talked her through riding the course effectively. I then had her ride this plan in her mind, visualize it, and also recite it verbally. She started to relax, and went into the ring and put in a very good performance.

Keri had developed a thinking habit when she was nervous, by which she was only able to visualize a negative outcome. It took about four shows, using the previously mentioned strategy, to break the fearful, negative habit. Keri was eventually able to come to the practice ring focused on riding in the present, with positive visualizations. For the first few shows, she had to be constantly reminded to trust her horse, her ability and her training, and to focus on feeling the horse under her and planning out her performance. When distracting thoughts – often negative – entered Keri's mind, she was asked to notice them, release them, and replace them by visualizing a plan which included paying attention to the rhythm and pace of her horse.

CREATING IMAGES

Visualization is a technique that enhances concentration and self-confidence. It improves concentration because it is an opportunity to practise it. Self-confidence is reinforced by visualization because it allows riders to plan out and practise performances prior to the actual performance. It is therefore especially important in practice and warm-up situations.

The results of visualization are truly phenomenal and its use is now being incorporated not only into sports training but into medicine, healing, and business. It has been found that the muscles, as well as the unconscious mind, cannot distinguish between visualized activity and actual activity. Sport psychology research has found that athletes who use visualization perform better than athletes who do not. The former are able to see, feel, and hear their performance in their mind. They can see themselves performing well from start to finish and accomplishing their goals.

There are two types of visualization, internal and external. Internal visualization entails riding in your mind's eye, as if you were actually doing it. External visualization is watching the images in your mind as if you were viewing a videotape of yourself. Internal visualization has been found to be much more effective than external visualization.

Visualization is a right-brain activity. It is similar to day-dreaming or playing make believe as a child. Since much of our formal schooling involves training and developing the left side of the brain (which is the analytical and logical side), it may take time for older riders to learn to tap into the creative right side of the brain. Classical music and relaxation training help stimulate the right side of the brain and enhance the ability to visualize, and anyone can learn the technique.

Visualizations are like vivid dreams. In order to learn to visualize effectively, first learn and use the relaxation exercise given on page 81. You must also make sure that you know specifically what you want to programme into your unconscious mind. Remember, the unconscious cannot distinguish between fantasy and reality. You do not want to programme garbage, or something that you are not sure you need. The next step is to plan out your visualization. First, choose a goal. Next, state the goal as a positive affirmation. Create the image in your mind as if it was already happening. Feel it happening as well as trying to see it. It may take a while for you to see it: just keep practising. Next, 'let go' of your visualization and affirm to yourself that you trust that you are able to create this. Remember, you cannot force things to happen. (Gawain, 1982).

Another technique that you may want to try involves writing out a statement on a card. For example:

Goal

I am riding in a relaxed and confident fashion, paying attention. My body feels energized and supple. My mind feels calm. I am thinking clearly. My mind and body are working together. They feel good and I feel relaxed and confident.

Place the card in front of you and focus on it for three minutes, then go through the relaxation exercise on page 81. When you get to 0, incorporate the visualization. Do this for two to three minutes. Then wake up by counting from one to five. Put the card in your pocket to view when needed.

MASTERY AND COPING REHEARSAL

Mastery and coping rehearsal are techniques designed to enhance concentration, confidence, and relaxation. These techniques train riders to develop their concentration by programming the mind to focus on the present and the task at hand. Mastery rehearsal involves visualizing a perfect performance. Coping rehearsal involves anticipating possible problems in a performance and coping successfully with those problems. Mastery and coping rehearsals work best when scripts are written and then recorded on an audio cassette with music in the background, and the tapes are listened to on a regular basis. Portable cassette players are convenient devices and can easily be taken to lessons and competitions. The principle is the same as listening to a song on the radio: the unconscious mind learns the words and does not have to strain to remember them.

Mastery and Coping Tapes

To make mastery and coping tapes you will need a tape recorder and a blank tape. Choose a competition or goal that you are preparing for and write it down. Next, write out your mental and physical training plans. List between three and five aspects that you want to work on. Be careful here: do not list too many. It is better to work on a few rather than too many because you do not want to overload your programme. Then, make a list that describes how you felt in the past when you performed well, or list how you think you need to feel in order to perform well. The elements in these lists go into the mastery script, which you will write out and then read into a tape recorder with your favourite background music playing.

Sample List for Mastery Script

Goal/Event preparing for:

Mental and physical training plans
1.

2.

3.

4.

5.

How I felt when I performed well in the past, or how I think I need to feel in order to perform well.

1.

2.

3.

4.

5.

How I ideally want the training and competition to go.

Pre-Competition (Two weeks before, one week before, three days before, morning of.)

1.

2.

3.

4.

5.

During Competition (go through elements of the entire competition).

1.

2.

3.

4.

5.

Sample Mastery Script

I am really excited about competing. My horse jumps 3 ft 6 in very well and is ready. The first show is in two weeks. I am riding five days a week, schooling him over jumps two days a week, working hard on the flat two days, and going for a relaxing walk one day a week. I am eating right, getting enough sleep, drinking lots of water, and doing my extra walking and stretching exercises.

My training is going well. I am practising my visualization and relaxation exercises every night, and whenever I feel anxious or stressed. When I find myself doubting my ability, I re-focus my attention on what I want to happen. During my visualization sessions I practise riding around the courses at the first show. I am able to feel my horse and his jumping. I am concentrating on riding each stride, in the present. I am working on keeping my pace and feel, and on keeping him going forward and straight.

It is now two days before the first day of the show. I am working on the flat, practising every movement, and focusing my attention on each stride. My horse is feeling very good and I am very confident. I am excited, and remind myself frequently to keep the excitement going outward. After my ride I clip my horse, then pack so that I am ready to leave tomorrow. I have checked all my tack and as I pack I am checking off the list all the equipment that I need to bring. I give my horse a big kiss and leave the yard.

I am now driving to the yard to meet the horsebox. I am feeling good and excited. Eating, sleeping, and working out has given me a physical edge. I have been getting up at 6 a.m. for the past few days, so that I have adjusted to the time I need to get up on my show days.

I check my equipment one last time, bandage my horse and put on his show halter. He looks great: he is in such good shape. We load him on the box, I get in my car, and we head for the show.

During the drive to the show I am listening to my favourite relaxing music. I am in the present, enjoying the drive on this beautiful spring day. As we arrive at the show, I wave to friends. My horse seems excited to be at the show. He loves competing so much. He is such an incredible athlete. I remind myself to focus in the present, and pay attention to him; to us as a team. He will help me out.

I tack him up and ride up to the ring to warm up and jump a few fences. I first do some stretching exercises, and am focusing on feeling my horse under me. I am focused on my horse and my schooling plans, leaving socializing for later. I go into the practice ring and walk around a few times to let him get comfortable. When I start trotting I focus on getting him going forward, and then on getting him to bend. He is feeling really good. I start cantering and can really feel the wonderful canter that he has. I practise moving forward at the canter down the long sides of the ring, and then balancing in the corner, without shortening the stride. He is really on form today.

My trainer comes out and instructs me to trot over the cross-pole. He feels so good, moving forward and springy. We jump it a few times and then my trainer sets up a vertical. We trot over this a few times, and then it is raised for him to canter over. He is feeling so good. I am seeing my distances miles away from the jump and reminding myself to trust what I see, relax, and follow his rhythm. Three fabulous jumps! Now it is time to school through a combination. He still feels great! I see my spot, over the first, two strides, and over the second. Land, balance and pull up. He is jumping out of his skin. I feel confident and relaxed. Now I'll take him for a long walk, then give him a bath, and organize everything for tomorrow morning.

I eat a good dinner and go back to my hotel and watch a movie. I am feeling relaxed and in the present. I practise my visualization before going to sleep.

Ring . . . ring; it is my 6 a.m. alarm call. I take a shower, dress, and go to the restaurant to get some breakfast. It is a beautiful morning. The temperature is just right, the spring air is good, and I am feeling strong and confident. As I arrive at the show at 7.30, the groom has just finished plaiting my horse. He looks so handsome. I give him a carrot, then tack him up and hop on. He needs lots of flatwork before the first class, and I have allowed forty-five minutes for this. He is working well. To make sure he is not too fresh I am pressing him a bit by extending the canter. He feels great. I walk for a while, go back to the stable to get my coat and number, and then return to school over jumps. He doesn't feel as though he needs a lot of jumping today – just enough to get us warmed up. I walk over and learn the first course. I watch the first horse go and am now memorizing the striding. I go back to the schooling ring and ride through the course without jumps. I am focusing my attention on each stride, balancing in the corners, pretending to see the spot I want to arrive at for each jump. I feel so relaxed and strong. By listening to the announcer I hear that I go in three horses time. I move up to the ring, and walk. I am now really planning how I want my ride to feel. I am confident, and I know the course. I am visualizing riding it, from walking into the ring, to getting the appropriate rhythm, and then tackling each fence.

As I walk into the ring I feel my horse grow about three inches. I say to him: 'Let's go and have fun, and you show them how great you are'. I pick up my trot immediately, circle, pick up the canter, and get him moving forward under me. As I turn the corner to the first jump on the diagonal, I immediately see the spot and realize I can just sit there; he meets the jump well, we land, I keep my leg on: one, two, three, four, leave the ground to jump number two; land, stride, stride, jump through the double. I focus on riding deep into the corner, balancing him while keeping his stride long; up to the outside line. As I come off the corner going forward I see a bit of a long stride so I ask him to extend a little to the jump; land, one, two, three, four, five, six, leave from a fabulous spot. Now I look to the end of the ring, ride deep into the corner, get my lead change and turn to the diagonal. The stride is there, trust, get to the jump well, one, two, three, four, five, six, seven, jump the oxer, land, look for the corner, balance and settle, and prepare for the last jump; a long gallop to an oxer. He is keeping the same pace; I focus on really feeling the rhythm, see the spot, trust it, and he jumps the last really well. I focus on the end of the ring, get my lead change, do my exit circle, and give my horse a big pat. He is very proud of himself.

Now, out to walk around and clear my head for the second round. I consult my trainer, who says 'That was wonderful'. I go and walk to let my horse rest a little, and as I do this I am memorizing the second course. I am also reminding myself to rest and 'let go' of that performance and focus in the present, on the new course. I need to get back to feeling like I did before the first course. I am confident that I will do so once I walk and rest a bit. I say 'thank you' to the compliments, but am not engaging in any conversations.

I am two horses away from going back in for the second course. I am feeling my energy level rise. We are ready. I keep walking, focusing on feeling each stride under me. We walk up to enter the ring, I say to my horse: 'Let's do it again' and we walk in and start trotting, make a circle, and pick up the canter. I am focused on feeling the pace, getting it right. This time it is a long gallop to the first jump, I see the spot, trust it – and sure enough it works – land, feel the stride under me as I go into the corner, ride out of the turn going forward to the upright on the diagonal; toward the double. Coming out of the turn I see a nice stride, trust it, and one, two, three, four to the double, one, two, and land to the corner, put my leg on to get him going forward, down the diagonal line. I see the next stride, jump, land; one, two, three, four, five, jump from a good spot, land, ride into the corner, and up the outside line. I check the first fence coming out of the corner, move up a little to it, land, one, two, three, four, five, six, jump, land, ride into the corner and find my last jump on the diagonal, relax, see the spot, and jump, land, and ride my exit circle. My horse was even better this time; he always gets better, even when I think he couldn't possibly go any better. He gets a huge pat and a kiss outside the ring. I hop off, throw a cooler on him, slip him a piece of carrot, and go for a walk to cool him down while I wait for the results to be announced. I can hardly believe my ears — we won both classes!

Now my job is to keep my head. I am so excited, but I have one more day of competition. I take my horse back to the stable, change my clothes, wash him, take out his plaits, rub his legs, rug him, and clean my tack. I remind myself to eat lunch and to visit some of my friends who are at the show. I decide to allow myself to come down from this surprise victory, and remind myself that it is not over yet. I will prepare for tomorrow, as I did for today.

Later in the afternoon, I take my horse out to graze, and I practise my visualization for tomorrow while he his munching. At 5 p.m. I feed him and go back to shower and have dinner. Then, watch another movie, visualization, and back to bed.

Next day I get my 6 a.m. wake-up call, shower, dress, go to the restaurant for breakfast, and arrive at the show at 7.30 a.m. It is another beautiful spring morning. I give my horse a few carrots and tack him up. Again, he looks great. I hop on forty-five minutes ahead of time and head for the schooling ring. He feels a little quieter today; I test him out and he *is* quiet, so I return to the stable, put on my coat and number and head back to the ring to learn the course. Today, I will have to focus on more leg to get him going forward. I am memorizing the course and trying to imagine the pace I'll need to get down the lines. I trot a little to warm up, practising extensions, and then canter, really getting him to work at moving forward. He feels good; I jump a few fences, and I'm ready. I practise visualizing and feeling the ride. Today I go first, so I am relying on trusting everything I have visualized. The announcer calls us to the ring. I touch his sides with my spurs, cluck and walk into the ring. I start to trot, survey my line, and then start cantering, asking him to move forward, which he does right off my leg. We come round the corner to the first jump, see a good distance, trust it, and jump; land, one, two, three, four, five, six; jump, land, ride into the corner. I make sure he is still moving forward, around the corner to the diagonal, see the spot, trust, jump, one, two, three, four, jump, land, one, two, jump; focus on getting him straight for the corner, deep into the turn, a little leg and spur; he is moving forward, see the spot for the first jump down the line, trust, one, two, three, four, five, six, seven, jump, land, ride the corner deep, and a nice lively gallop to the last oxer; see the stride, trust it, and leave from a great spot; land, focus on getting him straight, into the exit circle. We did it again! I give him a big pat and leave the ring, hop off him, and start walking him.

There is a long wait until the hack class. I take my horse back to the stable, let him rest and have some carrots. I have a snack and listen to music. With ten rounds left I go back to the ring for the hack class. They announce the results as I am going into the ring; my horse has won another class. OK, forget about it and focus on the class at hand. Since he is not a great mover, I have to work on making him look like the perfect hack. I find plenty of space and work at keeping it throughout the class. I've got him moving forward from behind and slightly flexed. He is such fun to ride; I am going to show the judge what a fun horse he is. We line up, and the judge announces the numbers to stay in. Wow! he is kept in. The other exhibitors continue and the judge calls two more horses in. We go back out and walk, trot, canter, and she calls us back in. We end up with a third. I am overjoyed. He is also Champion of the division.

Sample Coping Script

For the coping script you will need to make a list of three to five possible problems or distractions which you think you may encounter, and then list next to them ways that you can cope with them. When writing out your script, after the problem is encountered, include a statement where you tell yourself to relax, take a deep breath and count from 10 to 0, then include the coping response and talk yourself through working out the problem successfully.

The three elements of thought control are:

1. Recognize the problem and negative thoughts.
2. Say 'stop', relax, take a deep breath, count from 10 to 0.
3. Visualize the successful outcome.

It is 3 a.m. on the morning of the first day of the show. I am so nervous that I can hardly stand it. I can't believe I have woken up so early; I will be exhausted all day, which means I will not be able to ride well. *Stop, relax, take a deep breath, count backwards.* OK, now I'm feeling a little better. I know I can ride well on little sleep; sometimes I even ride better when I am tired. I can stand the nerves and do something about them. I will practise relaxation until I go back to sleep.

The phone rings at 6 a.m. I get up, shower, and go to breakfast. I am feeling OK. I drive to the show. Oh no, the groom has only just started plaiting and I need to get on in ten minutes to work my horse in. I'll never get him quiet in time. *Stop, relax, take a deep breath, count backwards.* OK, there is nothing I can do about this situation, except ask the groom to make big plaits. I can help her pull them up as she goes. I will get dressed and ready to go into the practise ring as soon as I get on. I will work my horse as hard as I can, and accept that it is the best I can do. I realize I must stay relaxed or he will get stronger. As I am getting ready I will practise relaxing; staying calm; stretching, and believing everything will work out.

I get on my horse and he doesn't feel too strong. I start working on the flat, making him work hard. I begin to school him over jumps and he trots his first fences nicely. I canter to a low vertical and he takes off, running into the corner. He has not had enough work; he might buck me off! *Stop, relax, regroup. Count backwards.* He will not buck me off. I need to remember to sit after landing and ride him up off his forehand. I can cope with this. I will ask the ring steward if I can be dropped down the order. No, he won't let me change. I go back to schooling: jumping, turning, and halting. I will let my horse stand for a while in the sun before going into the ring – that may quieten him down.

We are now going in for the first round. My horse still feels strong. I can cope with this. I must ride him soft and forward. Going to the first jump I see a good stride; he jumps well, and is rideable down the line: 'Oh no, on landing he gets strong'. *Relax, breathe, keep his stride long through the corner and his head up.* We made it, turning to the diagonal line he relaxes; I see a good stride and he jumps well; down to the double – he jumps it super, but is strong on landing. *Relax, breathe, get him straight, and keep the stride long.* It worked; he is relaxing again going down the outside line. This time, sit on landing; there, I did it, he is settling into the corner, now he is relaxing more, round the corner to the last fence; I see a good spot and he jumps it well, and lands nicely. Wow, I coped with this situation!

9

Concentration

One of the most basic tenets of mental training is that the mind operates most efficiently when you focus your attention on what you want to happen; exactly how you want to perform. This is a very simple concept, yet the reality is that it can be very difficult to do consistently. A major difficulty in applying this concept often arises when riders focus too much of their attention on distractions. One common distraction is focusing too much attention on the results of performance and trying to control them, rather than focusing on the process that is involved in creating a successful performance. Difficulties also arise when riders do not know what the actual process is.

Concentration is the ability to pay attention to something. It is a misunderstood concept because often riders feel that they either have the ability to concentrate or they do not. However, concentration does not work that way. Everyone has the ability to concentrate, although sometimes people have trouble concentrating on what they are supposed to be doing, or would like to. In riding, it is important to teach riders *exactly* what to focus on. Trainers often encourage their riders to 'concentrate' but, if the rider does not know exactly what they are supposed to be paying attention to, then it is impossible for them to do so.

Anxiety and various distractions cause concentration errors. Competitive stress and pressure interfere with concentration because riders' foci of attention are often distracted by thoughts that are irrelevant to performance. They may be concentrating on thoughts about how nervous their body feels, or thoughts, fears or questions regarding their ability to execute a skill; the competition, or how they want to win the class; or hoping that they can remember an exercise or course, which is essentially concentrating on their lack of self-confidence. Even the realization that you are doing well during a performance can distract your attention from it!

FOCUSING ATTENTION

Errors or lapses in concentration occur when riders pay attention to distractions rather than to what they want to happen. They may be paying attention to things going on outside the ring, such as other riders, or thinking that the ring or jumps are too big. In this case, the attention span has become too broad. To correct this, the rider must focus on what is happening in the present moment and narrow their span of attention.

When riders pay too much attention to their own thoughts about what is going on in their own mind or body, their attention span becomes too narrow. For example, riders may be distracted by feeling nervous if they choose to pay attention to their feelings of nervousness rather than focusing on what they are doing.

Many riders feel nervous yet perform well in spite of their feelings. Effective concentration entails learning how to read the attentional demands of the present situation, in order that you may determine what to include in your thoughts and what to exclude, as well as maintaining a present focus. Development of this skill, called focus of attention, is outlined in the following case study.

Nancy

Nancy, a professional exhibitor of hunters and jumpers, who also trains several juniors, found that when she was showing she was distracted by the pressure of training the junior riders. Nancy felt that her riding performance suffered from her inability to focus in on her different jobs. She frequently felt confused and out of control. The solution to Nancy's problem was teaching her to identify the things that she needed to focus on whilst showing, and to forget about the juniors, and vice versa. We wrote out a job description for each position, and identified the attentional cues that she needed to focus on in order to perform effectively in each position. Nancy also learned to set up boundaries for each job. She asked the juniors and their parents to refrain from talking to her about their business while she was competing, so that she could focus. She set up specific times for business matters, teaching, and riding, so that her days had more structure. This gave her a time for each aspect of her job, which helped her to focus.

What is important to learn from such tendencies is that riders can do some self-study and determine what it feels like when they are able to concentrate, and what it feels like when their concentration becomes too narrow or too broad. They can learn to make adjustments, which means learning to pay attention to larger or smaller areas of the ring as well as paying more or less attention to what is going on with their own bodies. Riders can improve their concentration by learning to focus on, and simulate in their minds, flowing performances – which will help them to re-focus when they are distracted. The key here is learning to recognize the distracting thoughts, then relaxing the mind by using the following technique to focus on the present and the task at hand, to visualize the successful outcome and later, after the performance, to work on identifying and changing attitudes, beliefs, and thoughts which are causing problems.

In this series of pictures Abigail Lufkin, 1999 bronze medallist at the Pan Am games, demonstrates total focus. Her eyes and body position exude confidence and concentration.

Exercise: Developing Attentional Focus

In order to focus in the present first practise this relaxation exercise. Sit or lie down in a comfortable position. Start taking deep breaths, inhaling through your nose and exhaling through your mouth. Next, focus on your breathing and begin counting from 50 to 0 on each exhalation: 50, 49, 48, 47, 46, 45, 44, 43, 42, 41, 40 . . . continuing to count down to zero. After you reach zero, start again at 50. Learning to concentrate involves relaxing the mind and paying attention to the appropriate demands of the present situation. Practise this relaxation exercise at least three times a day. You will find that each time relaxation occurs faster. Count from 0 to 5 to wake yourself up.

WHAT TO CONCENTRATE ON

Developing concentration entails learning to concentrate on one thing at a time. When you first get on a horse, loosen up and get the feel of the horse; follow the horse's balancing gestures (the back and forth movements of his head and neck) with your hands for a minute or two at the walk and do some stretching exercises to get the right feel. This brings the focus of attention in the present moment. Think about what is happening now. Make this part of your practice routine. While you have a mental plan of what is to be accomplished, your attention is on what is happening now. Pay attention to, and live in, the 'now', so that you will be in the present when you perform.

When irrelevant thoughts distract concentration, focus on:

- Paying attention to the present.
- Identifying what you need to focus on.
- Getting the feel and pace back.
- Making sure the horse is moving forward and straight.
- Developing a routine in which you visualize or imagine the way that you want the horse to feel.

Stick with this procedure even if you do not achieve the desired result after the first or second try. As you gain experience, this practice can help you regain your concentration faster and more easily. These practice exercises can be incorporated into training sessions.

To narrow your attention, try concentrating on a small object, such as a freckle or the second hand of your watch. Focus all of your attention on it for one minute. To broaden your attention, focus your eyes as far as they can see; then turn your head from left to right.

Other exercises which help to develop focus are:

- Stretching on the horse.
- Walking and trotting with your eyes closed.
- Focusing on following the balancing gestures of the horse at the walk and canter.
- Riding without stirrups.
- Cavalletti and gridwork exercises.
- Reminding yourself to focus on each stride.
- Focusing on the stride immediately after a jump.

Internal thought processes which may distract your attention include:

- Thinking about results.
- Thoughts about what others are thinking.
- Thoughts about how tense your body is.
- Thoughts about the past or future, especially past errors such as errors at previous jumps.
- Thoughts about what you fear *might* happen (stop, spook, missed change of lead, etc.).

To conquer such mental distractions, develop self-talk that will effectively re-focus your attention. You can do this by focusing your attention back on what your *want* to happen. Before you ride, you can jot that down on a small piece of paper and put it in your pocket. Look at it whenever you become distracted.

PRACTICE AND CONCENTRATION

The ability to concentrate is enhanced by practising in the same way as you want to perform. For example, if your performance involves jumping eight fences with broken lines, practise that, rather than just jumping two fences, or working on combinations. Practise riding the course on the flat before you go into the ring. The duration of concentration that is practised should equal the duration required in the competition. The aim is to perform what you *know* you can do, and have practised. If you cannot actually practise, watch videos of what you are going to be performing.

Often, the 'hurry up and wait' aspect of performing in many equestrian disciplines causes riders difficulty with concentration. Remember, when you feel rushed, that you have more time than you think you have. While being respectful of the collecting ring steward, remind yourself that you can take a deep breath and take your time. Give yourself the opportunity to regain your focus. Your goal is to perform your best; the ring steward's goal is to keep the show running, thus performing his best.

Long waits tend to disturb your energy level. When you find that there is going to be a delay, give yourself a mental break. Remember that you have no control over the delay, and that patience is part of competing. Relax, and when it is time, use self-talk to re-energize yourself. By practising for these aspects of competition, you will gain a mental advantage.

Concentration can also be enhanced by watching and focusing on the performance of others. Make sure however, that you watch others who are performing well. One phenomenon that I have observed and experienced at horse shows is that if there is a refusal, fall, or problem at a certain jump, often the following competitors will have the same problem. Many times it is not a problem with the jump; it occurs because the riders waiting to go watched the wrong thing. They unknowingly developed the wrong mental picture in their minds. When competing it is beneficial to concentrate on your strengths and your best performances.

THREATS TO CONCENTRATION

In order to retain your concentration in all circumstances, it helps to be forewarned of situations which may challenge your ability to concentrate. The sooner you can identify a potential threat, the sooner you can re-focus.

Psych-outs

Sometimes, competitors think that 'psyching out' their rivals will give them a competitive advantage. More often than not these attempts at psych-outs backfire. They cause breaks in concentration because the focus is taken off the task at hand and placed on schemes that involve mind games with the rivals, or manipulation. In order to handle others' attempts at psyching you out, you must focus only on your performance, not what they are doing or saying. Also, instead of getting angry because someone is attempting to psych you out, get excited because *you now know* that they are probably hurting their own performance by losing their focus as well as being worried that you can beat them.

Slumps

A slump can be defined as a temporary drop in performance. Slumps have a major affect on concentration and self-confidence. They are sometimes rooted in technical problems, technical changes or flaws, fatigue, changes in performance level and injuries. While they seem as if they might last forever, in reality they will not. Slumps affect concentration because they cause riders to think more about the slump than the actual performance, which focuses attention on the problem with the technique, rather than the solution. They can cause riders to become depressed because they feel helpless with regard to improving their performance.

The most important thing to remember about slumps is that they *do not* last forever: there is a future beyond the slump. Great patience is needed to cope with a slump – do not set a time limit on recovery. Also, consider that the slump may be a signal that it is time to 'take a breather' and rest. It is important for riders to stay positive during slumps and remind themselves each day that today could be the day that it breaks and, if it is not, then they are still one day closer to the end of the slump.

Regaining Concentration After a Bad Performance

Bad performances wreak havoc with the ability to concentrate because the mind seems to prefer to focus on the bad performance and replay it. When bad performances occur it is important to recognize your mistakes and then let go of the performance. The mind must concentrate on *correcting* the mistakes and on how to achieve flowing performances. At this point it may be worthwhile watching videos of best performances, or using visualization to focus on what you *can* do rather than on what happened.

PERFORMANCE ROUTINES

Performance routines motivate riders and focus their attention. They give riders a feeling of security because they have a plan.

Specific performance routines can be designed for each rider, but be sure to include the following elements in yours:

- A specific time to start.
- A brief relaxation technique (deep breaths, count backwards 10–0).
- Visualization of the performance (pre-practice) and successful outcome.
- A focus word, such as 'Intensity'.

For example, when there are two horses in front of you, stretch out your arms and legs, take several deep breaths, remind yourself to focus in the present, decide on three elements of the performance to focus on, and then visualize the performance – that is, ride it in your mind, imagining a successful outcome.

Sample Performance Routine

Two horses in front of me – walk, allowing my hands to follow the movement of my horse's head and neck, and mentally psych up or relax, depending on my intensity level.

One horse in front of me – visualize entrance, then the entire ride, feeling each step.

Entering the ring – turn on showmanship. Quick feeling of intensity, eyes up, shoulders back, develop pace, focus self and horse on the first jump or movement.

Incorporate performance routines into every practice session and every competitive situation so that they become automatic. They will enhance your positive thinking and feelings of control, no matter what the situation may entail.

Performance routine worksheet

My performance routine will start:

I will check my intensity level at (time):

Intensity Check. The psych-up or relaxation technique I will use is:

(example: deep breaths, count backward 10–0).

Immediately prior to my performance I will visualize my performance (pre-practice) and my successful outcome.

My focus word is:

At the arena entrance I will:

Note: I will practise my routine while schooling and use it before each performance. I will make adjustments when necessary.

Exercise: Focus, Concentration and Performance

1. When competing, what type of concentration errors do you tend to experience? List ways by which you can bring your concentration into the appropriate focus.

2. When performing, do you tend to get too far ahead or too far behind your performance mentally?

3. List three methods that you can incorporate into your training regime that will remind you to focus on the present.
   (i)

   (ii)

   (iii)

4. Design a performance routine.

Remember, it is very important to simulate your mental and physical routine in practice, in order for it to work in competition. It is also important to commit yourself to practising in the way you want to perform.

10

At the Competition

Did you ever take a maths test in school and find that all the questions seemed different from those that your teacher had taught you? It may be that the test was to see how well you could apply the *theory*. This same feeling can happen in competition. You have prepared at home, and now you are being asked to apply what you have learned in a new setting under different conditions. You can prepare mentally by knowing how to answer the questions that the course is asking, so first you must assess the course.

PREPARING TO RIDE COURSES OR TESTS

Preparing to ride a course or a test well involves memorizing it and then developing a plan to ride it with reference to the horse that you have on that day. Therefore, it is also necessary to memorize and visualize your *plan*.

Memorizing the Course
Many riders complain that they cannot remember the course. You must first *believe* that you can memorize the course – and anyone can do

this. It just takes practice. Since people tend to learn in different ways, you may try different ways until you find one with which you are comfortable. Some riders can learn the course from the posted course chart by reading it over several times. If you do it this way then you must read the course chart until you *know* it. When riders are nervous they have the tendency to be impatient and want to hurry things along. Others riders feel more comfortable writing the course down on a piece of paper until they feel that they know it. For others, it may be easier to learn the course by having someone talk them through it several times, while others yet may need to watch it ridden. When trying to learn a dressage test or a cross-country course for which you have the layout in advance, you may find it helpful to record it into a tape recorder and then listen to it several times. If you have the opportunity to walk the course, it is probably most helpful to learn it from the map first, so that when you are walking it you can concentrate on developing a plan to ride it, or walk the course more than once. If you have a trainer instructing you and other riders while walking the course, get up close so you can focus your attention on what is being said and take notes if you cannot remember everything.

You can also practise writing out your own courses and memorizing them at home.

Developing Your Plan

This involves being able to read the requirements of the course (distances, jump heights, widths, etc.) and making a plan that is suitable for your horse according to his ability and level of training. The challenge here is to be analytical and figure out how you must ride your horse to execute the course successfully. When planning your ride, you must take into consideration the variations of terrain, the size and shape of the ring, the depth of the corners, the type of jumps, and the relationship between each obstacle and those preceding and following. (For example, oxer to oxer; oxer to vertical; vertical to oxer; oxer to combination; water; long gallop to a single fence; broken line; sharp turn). You must know the distances between fences and the pace at which your horse can make those distances, keeping in mind that how a line rides depends on how you jumped into it. For example, if the lines are set on a 12 ft stride and your horse has a 14 ft stride, you will know that you will have to balance and shorten his stride to make the distances. You will have to know the pace at which he covers the ground in approximately 12 ft strides. A vertical to oxer line will ride longer than an oxer to oxer or oxer to vertical line. If you jump into a vertical line big then it will ride shorter than if you jump into the line from a deep stride. You can practise these different distances at home to get comfortable with them. You may also want to give thought to riding any given line in three different ways; if your horse jumps in from a long, medium, or close spot, so you know the appropriate adjustments to make. You can practise this when schooling at home with poles on the ground. However, because the way you jump into a line at any time will affect the way it rides, it is always extremely important to be focused in the present, riding each stride.

There are other adaptations you may have to make on the spur of the moment, which will be assisted by prior thought and preparation. For example, you may need to know how your horse's stride changes when he is nervous or tired. Does it become longer or shorter? How does he handle hard ground as opposed to mud or deep going?

When analysing the course and making your plan you need to take into consideration changes in terrain and type of jump. In addition to the horse's stride length changing when going uphill or downhill, his balance may change also. For example, when riding uphill to a fence you may need more leg and less hand and, downhill, a little more hand to balance him — and you may also need to concentrate on staying over his centre of balance, which is right behind the shoulder.

Changes in type of jump may also have an effect on your and the horse's concentration, so you should include in your plan which part of the obstacle to focus your joint attention on. For example, when jumping a wide fence you need to pick the spot where you want your horse to jump it and set him up to focus on that spot. If you don't, he may be looking all over the place or drifting to one side. When jumping a very narrow fence, you have less room for error and much more room for a run-out or refusal, so you must narrow your attention and get your horse set up to lock onto the centre of the fence, and ride it very boldly.

(When going from a difficult obstacle to an easier one it is quite common to make a mistake because you ease off somewhat, and lose some of your focus. Therefore, you may want to remind yourself to remain psyched up for the easy obstacle after the tough one.)

When planning your ride around a course remember to make specific plans for keeping your pace, balance and rhythm through the turns. You may want to remind yourself to work immediately on regaining your balance, pace, and rhythm after each jump by maintaining your feel through the leg and rein aids. It is the flatwork that makes the jumps good: even the best jumpers in the world have a hard time if the flatwork is poor!

Finally, note changes in energy level or intensity that you may need to make because your horse is becoming tired. Make plans for increasing your energy level (or reducing it) when necessary. For example, you may find that you need more strength and energy around the corners to maintain your pace and to ride your horse forward out of the corners than you do going down the lines. You may find that you get tired three-quarters of the way round a course, and that your horse's stride length changes when he is tired: that is when you think 'energy'. Include in your plans a spot where you can take a little breather for a second or two, and literally breathe while focusing on the next jump. You may want to tell yourself to relax, while keeping the pace, in the corners.

In summary, you have two jobs when preparing to ride the course. The first is to memorize it and the second is to develop a plan and then visualize and feel yourself executing that plan until you are totally confident to attack the course and ride it like a champion, focusing on what you want to happen. Most of success comes from preparation, with a little luck thrown in.

PREPARATION FOR A THREE-DAY EVENT

All the phases of the three-day event have become more challenging in recent years. The dressage tests require a precision that is achieved through concentration, training and controlling the movement of the horse – lengthening, shortening, and balancing. Designers of cross-country courses have introduced combinations, lines, bends and angles which test the horse's and rider's technical ability to adjust not only to the conditions of the terrain, but to the obstacles and distances. Most showjumping courses are now built to test the rider's ability to adjust to technical demands. Mental preparation is therefore necessary in order for you to adjust yourself and your horse to the challenges of the various phases.

Overall, each phase tests the rider's ability to balance, lengthen, and shorten the horse. Part of mental training entails designing plans for training the horse for all the phases. Often, I see three-day event riders focusing most of their attention on getting their horse fit enough to complete the cross-country course. In competition, their focus, too, is mainly on the cross-country phase. It is easy to understand their concerns – the courses can be very challenging. In order to be competitive though, it is necessary to be mentally and physically prepared for *all* the phases.

The work that you put in on balancing, lengthening and shortening your horse's stride for the dressage movements will help you to handle the cross-country phase better. Being able to gallop on, and then balance and shorten your horse's stride to ride through a combination, and then lengthen and accelerate again are skills that often separate the winners from the also-rans. The skills come from good flatwork. You can design training plans in which you practise the dressage movements and apply them to the cross-country phase. If practising flatwork is not your favourite occupation, then doing so as preparation for the cross-country and showjumping phases may provide an added incentive!

The Dressage Test

When three-day event riders tell me that they are no good at dressage, I suggest to them that making that area their strength should be one of their goals. If you are such a rider, rather than leaving the dressage test to the last minute, start practising as early as possible. Take lessons from a dressage expert, and have them help you turn your weakness into your strength. Several weeks prior to the event, begin daily practice by visualizing the test. Practise the rhythm and balance, shortening and lengthening the stride in your mind. Practise each movement in the test, from start to finish, in your mind. You can also practise correcting any disobediences that you might encounter. Finally, practise attaining the level of intensity or energy that you require in order to ride a good test.

Robert Stevenson and *Risky Business* representing Canada in the dressage phase of the 1992 Olympic Three-Day Event.

If you do this, you will find that, when test day comes you are much more comfortable in the dressage arena. Remember, focus on *what you want to happen*. If you think that your horse is no good at dressage, or that this phase is not so important, that is the result you will get. If you want to improve your dressage, focus on that intention, practise and prepare, and you *will* improve.

Riding a dressage test requires a narrower focus of attention than riding the cross-country or showjumping course. The focus is also more internal because you must be thinking quickly about the movement you are performing, and also preparing for the next one. There is not much time to rest or go blank. Therefore, when you are preparing to ride the test, you want to practise mentally narrowing your attention to the size of the dressage arena. Visualize, as well as practise, riding the test in an arena of the correct size. The only thing on your mind should be riding the test; getting the feel of the horse that you require. Since this type of focus requires a quiet mind, you may find that when you (or your horse) are feeling nervous it is helpful to use the relaxation exercise in Chapter 8 prior to performing. If you find yourself distracted by other people, horses, sights, or sounds, it is an indication that your focus is too broad. Concentrate on yourself and your horse. Narrow your vision by staring at his ears, and focus on what you want to happen – your plan for riding the test.

Once in the arena, *ride* the entire test, stride by stride. The mental error that many riders make is that they give up really riding the test if their horse is not perfect (too strong, distracted, etc.) at the beginning. To improve the consistency of your performance, focus your attention on riding each stride, getting into the flow of your performance, and continue riding throughout the entire test. Even when your horse is performing poorly, focus on the whole test rather than becoming distracted by the horse's behaviour. You will find that you finish better than you started, and you can build on that for your next dressage performance. You will also be effectively preparing the horse better for riding the cross-country course.

The Cross-country

Your first task in preparing to ride the cross-country course is to walk it and develop a plan to ride it. This plan should include the pace necessary to jump each obstacle and the angle of approach. When walking the course, it may be helpful to take a pen and paper with you so that you can make notes from which you can work out your plan of attack.

Your mental task, when riding the course, is to help your horse focus on each obstacle as you are approaching it, and to concentrate on clearing it. You can help him by knowing the best pace from which to jump each obstacle, and preparing him to achieve that pace. This is what you should visualize, over and over again, before the actual ride. If you go out with the attitude 'I'm not sure what will happen', your ride will reflect that attitude. Another part of your task is to maintain your focus and level of intensity throughout the course. Since it will take longer than the dressage or showjumping phases, you must be able to concentrate for a longer period of time, and this is something else you can practise in advance.

Some riders have the tendency of 'letting down' after the hardest obstacle(s) on the course, and this sometimes causes a problem at an easier one. The 'sigh of relief' causes riders to lose their concentration, and make silly mistakes. To correct this tendency, think of each jump as being as important as every other one – they all carry the same penalties – and remind yourself to ride the whole course. Save the sigh of relief for after you have crossed the finishing line!

There is also a tendency for riders to 'let down' after the cross-country phase itself. This is easily understood because, by this point in the competition, a lot of mental and physical fatigue has built up. This causes a 'flat' feeling, which may actually be harder to overcome than nerves. I've noticed that three-day event riders take incredible care of their horses' physical needs after the cross-country, but often at the expense of their own needs. To overcome some of the fatigue and put in a good showjumping performance you need to eat, drink, and rest. Therefore, include plans for your own recovery when planning your strategy for the event. You may want to bring nutritious food with you; sport drinks; good water, and a trusted groom to care for your horse while you rest.

Paying attention to the following points will help you to overcome 'flatness' and re-energize yourself for the final phase.

- Drink plenty of water.
- Get as much sleep as possible.
- Eat . . . preferably healthy, energizing food.
- Think Energy!
- Visualize creating the level of intensity/energy that you want for the final phase.
- When rested, review you plans for the final phase.

The Showjumping Course

Anne Kursinski says that a showjumping course demands 'bravery, carefulness, scopiness, speed, and adjustability [of the horse]; from the rider, it demands skilful analysis, strategic thinking, quick responses, and effective riding'. Three out of four of these rider requirements are mental. I have already talked about assessing the course, visualizing it, and the importance of preparing yourself and the horse to tackle the course 'in the present'. In the context of three-day eventing it is important, during your assessment and preparation, that you bear in mind the possibility that your horse may be somewhat tired during the showjumping. Alternatively, if he was 'lit up' by the previous day's cross-country, he may be somewhat 'buzzy'. Either way – or even if he reacts exactly as you expected – tackling the course 'in the present' is the key: you must ride the horse as you find him.

RESPONDING TO MENTAL CHALLENGES

When the Course Looks Unmanageable

Some riders, when they first look at a course, think 'I can't do this, it is unmanageable'. When you have such thoughts, focus your mind back on what you *want* to happen. You may use the word 'bravery' as a focus, or say to yourself 'I want to ride around this course successfully'; 'I can manage it', and go to work on your plan. The course may seem more manageable if you break it down to learn it. For example, ask yourself 'Can I clear the first jump? Yes'. Then 'Can I ride the next jump? Yes', and so on. Once you have got yourself around that way, you can then start to practise riding the entire course. Above all else, remember to keep your mind positive, and keep the focus on rising to the challenge!

When the Jumps Look Huge
Sometimes, when you are nervous or in a new situation, the jumps can look really big. This is a common psychological reaction, especially when you are walking the course and not sitting high up on your horse. One rider who I work with reminds herself that they look smaller when she is on her horse, and this alleviates the distraction and fear. You can also remind yourself that the fences are no bigger than the specifications for the class, and the fact that they are looking bigger is in your mind. Use the relaxation technique presented earlier (page 73) to calm your mind down, and continue to remind yourself that the fences are within the designated height and width standards, which you have prepared for. Rather than focusing on their size, visualize yourself jumping them. If you can't do that, first visualize someone else jumping them effortlessly, then visualize yourself jumping them effortlessly.

Remind yourself that the extra adrenalin boost that you get from nerves can actually give you the energy you need to jump the big fences, and make sure to stretch out your muscles and warm up until you feel that you are loose and energized.

The Spooky Jump
Preparing mentally for a spooky jump involves convincing yourself that it is *not* spooky, and riding down to it in a strong manner, with

this conviction in your mind. The more you buy into the spook, the more your horse will sense your fear and act in a spooky way. The spooky jump is one that really tests your effectiveness as a rider, both mentally and physically. Numerous champion competition horses are spooky, but their riders have learned to ride them effectively.

When you first enter the ring, it may be possible to give your horse a look at the spooky jump. You should do this in an assertive manner, communicating to your horse: 'See, this is OK.' Looking may also give you a better view of how you will ride down to the fence in question. The tougher you are mentally, the better your horse will go.

The Jump Your Horse Dislikes

Some riders develop the belief that their horse dislikes a certain type of fence. While he may do so, you cannot mentally buy into his dislike. The more you buy into the horse's fear, the more likely he is to stop at the jump. Riders also tend to avoid doing what their horse does not like, when doing the opposite – practising it more – is what will solve the problem. Devise a plan to make the horse's weakness his strength and, at the same time, stay mentally focused on what you want to happen. For example, you want to focus on teaching your horse to like water jumps, rather than focusing on the belief that he dislikes them. I often see riders get so locked into what their horse likes and doesn't like that it inhibits their riding progress and effectiveness. I even see them continue to focus on the problem after it is solved! For example, when your horse was a youngster in his first year of competition he may have disliked water, but now he is a ten-year-old veteran, he likes it. Some riders are still thinking that their horse is having a problem when he has actually grown out of it – the rider must, too! Practise and prepare more for the weakness than the strength, with a positive, open mind.

The Spectre of Results

As I have stressed throughout this book, forget about the results. Only pay attention to results if it really helps you to do so. For most riders, it creates too much pressure. Focus on riding each phase as best you can, regardless of what position you are in. When your goal is your own peak performance, it does not matter what position you are in. You will do your best and the results, over which you have no control, will take care of themselves.

Dressage Worksheet

1. Write out the test
2. Draw the test
3. List of movements that I do well:

4. Movements that I need to work on:

5. I will work on my weakness when . . .
6. I will ride the entire test — times prior to competition on days . . .
7. I will practise visualizing the test daily

Cross-country Worksheet

1. Draw up sheet for walking the course
2. Formulate plan for riding each jump — balance, lengthen, line of approach etc.
3. Work out time plans: where to be on course at what time.
4. List mental reminders — ride whole course, focus on energy, etc.

Sample Pre/Post-Competitive Checklist
(Circle the answer that best describes your performance.)

Position and Controls

Were my eyes up?	Yes	No
Were my shoulders square?	Yes	No
Did I maintain balance?	Yes	No
Did I follow the horse's balancing gestures?	Yes	No
Did I feel the horse?	Yes	No
Did I maintain the rhythm?	Yes	No
Did I have the correct pace?	Yes	No
Did I have the correct leg position?	Yes	No
Did I use my hands correctly?	Yes	No
Did I use my weight correctly?	Yes	No

Evaluate how I jumped the fences _____

_____

_____

_____

Physical Condition

Breathing	Relaxed	Tight	
Muscular Tension	Low	Moderate	High
Energy Level	Low	Moderate	High
Arousal Level	Low	Optimal	Too high
Muscular Strength	Low	Moderate	High
Muscular Flexibility	Low	Moderate	High
Did I eat well?	Yes	No	
Did I drink enough?	Yes	No	
Did I get enough sleep?	Yes	No	

Emotional Control

Did I feel self-confident?	Yes	No	
Did I use positive self-talk?	Yes	No	
Did I use negative self-talk?	Yes	No	
Did I control my anger?	Yes	No	Not applicable
Was I able to control my nerves?	Yes	No	
Did I choke?	Yes	No	
Did I blame others for my mistakes?	Yes	No	
Did I feel jealous?	Yes	No	
Did I feel envious?	Yes	No	
Did I compare of myself to others	Yes	No	
Emotionally I felt:	Good	Bad	OK

Mental Training Strategies

Did I formulate daily performance goals/plans?	Yes	No
Did I execute my planned goals?	Yes	No
Did I ride with a present focus?	Yes	No
Did I trust what I had practised?	Yes	No
Did I use my performance routine?	Yes	No
Did I use visualization?	Yes	No
Did I adjust my energy level?	Yes	No

Concentration

Did I remember the course?	Yes	No
Did I remember the striding?	Yes	No
Was I able to ride the strides?	Yes	No
Did I use my corners effectively?	Yes	No
Did I remember my plan?	Yes	No
Did I execute my plan?	Yes	No

Distraction Control Strategies

I was able to turn stress into challenge	Yes	No
I was able to 'let go' of mistakes	Yes	No
I focused on positive aspects of performance	Yes	No
I evaluated performance, when leaving the competition arena, in a positive manner	Yes	No
I accepted my performance	Yes	No

My distractions were _____

My reactions were _____

I can improve my reactions by _____

Performance Outcomes

My performance was: (circle one)

Peak performance

Consistent high performance

Consistent average performance

Inconsistent performance

My strengths were:

My weaknesses were:

I will commit to:

1. Praising myself for my strengths.
2. Letting go of my mistakes.
3. Accepting my performance.
4. Identifying positive practice methods.
5. Congratulating myself for competing.

Signed _____

Date _____

11

Getting the Basics Right

If there was only one piece of advice I could give to riders it would be *master the basics*. What that means is learn about the horse – his temperament, his movement, his talent, his ability, and learn how to communicate with him. Horses respond to positive communication. A big part of that is your mental outlook and ability to control your emotions – which is what this book is about – but the second aspect of communication is how you communicate with the horse through your position and the use of your aids.

THE NEED FOR CORRECT TECHNIQUE

Riders become frustrated, angry, and fearful when there is a block between what they want to do and what the horse will do. While this obstacle is sometimes created when the rider has a mental block, it occurs at other times when the rider's position or aids are incorrect or ineffective. *It is important to understand that all the positive thinking in the world will not overcome*

You are never too young or too old to work on the basics. Here, seven-year-old Katherine Newman shows how it is done!

communication problems between you and your horse caused by misuse or abuse of your aids, or a position that interferes with the horse's movement.

There are many good books available which deal with understanding the horse and developing the basic position and controls. Suggested reading includes Anne Kursinski's *Riding and Jumping Clinic, The de Nemethy Method, Riding Logic* by Muesler, *Common Sense Horsemanship* by Littauer, and George Morris's books. In *That Winning Feeling!* Jane Savoie presents a good explanation of how to use your aids effectively. Video tapes are also excellent learning tools. However, while books and tapes can give you the mental picture and understanding, they are not substitutes for a good instructor and a good horse to learn from.

To develop into a good rider, you must cultivate patience with yourself, your instructor, and your horses. You may see the professionals at the shows making riding look effortless, but the reality is that becoming an effective rider involves time, energy, and hard work focused on mastery of the rider's basic position and the flatwork.

DEALING WITH TRAINING PROBLEMS

When you encounter a problem, rather than reacting with anger, frustration and impatience, view the problem as a challenge. Go back to the basics:

1. What am I thinking?
2. Am I using my position and aids correctly and consistently?

Next, visualize doing it right, then try again!

Common Causes of Anger and Frustration
There are very few bad horses. Horses generally get labelled as bad when they are actually misunderstood, and their riders do not use the correct position and aids. The horse picks up on the confusion, anger, and frustration that the rider is feeling, and reacts in the same way himself. The following is a list of situations that commonly cause anger and frustration.

When the rider is over-horsed, under-horsed, or otherwise improperly mounted

- Poor position
- Poor use of aids
- Conflicting aids
- When rider becomes fearful

- When rider does not know how to handle disobedience or freshness
- Making the same mistake over and over again
- Undiagnosed physical problems in the horse
- Lack of physical condition in rider
- Competing at the wrong level
- Politics in judged competition
- Lack of knowledge
- Lack of experience
- Lack of time for proper training
- Inconsistent performance

Dealing with Anger and Frustration

While the causes of anger and frustration can vary, the responses are usually quite similar – some type of strong emotional reaction. The key in learning to handle anger is identifying what is causing you to lose patience and to react emotionally, then finding an effective way of handling the situation. For example, if your horse is being disobedient, find a trainer to help you. The trainer may discover that you are using your aids improperly, and help you to learn the correction and resolve the problem.

When you are really angry, take the time to step back, take a few deep breaths, use the relaxation exercise (page 73) and focus on solving the problem. Visualize working the problem out. Focus hard on using the proper aids. Be kind and patient with yourself. If you find that you are unable to let go of the anger, write about it. It has been found that writing about your anger helps you to release it.

Frustration occurs when there are obstacles in the way of achieving your goal. You react emotionally to the obstacles, and the mind seems to shut down its creative ability to overcome them. However, frustration can be overcome in much the same way as anger. Use the relaxation exercise to calm the mind, then think creatively. Look for new ways to overcome the problem. Read books, listen to motivational tapes, or talk to others who have been in

Jessie Keeney reminds us to have FUN!

similar situations. Frustration seems to narrow your focus, so you want to open it up to new possibilities.

Exercise: Dissipating Anger

1. Describe the situation that caused you to become angry or frustrated.

2. Do the relaxation exercise. When you feel relaxed, visualize, on each exhalation, letting go of the anger. You can visualize it going out into the air; into the ground; or into a river. Make a decision to let go of the anger.

3. List some ways whereby you can solve the problem the next time it happens. Then, visualize yourself reacting in a calm, effective manner and working through the problem.

12

Factors Affecting Physical and Psychological Condition

The physical condition of the rider contributes to peak performance. Riders in excellent physical shape tend to handle the physical and psychological stresses of competition better than riders who are not in good shape. Since riding requires some degree of aerobic fitness, muscular strength and muscular flexibility, those who are not able to ride enough to maintain their fitness level may benefit from supplementing their training with aerobic, weight, and flexibility work.

SLEEP

Sleep plays an important role in the physical condition of the rider. Although horse show schedules may be gruelling, learning to get enough sleep and napping when possible will improve performance by helping prevent fatigue. Lack of sleep causes concentration problems, and affects coordination and reaction time. When sleep cycles are disturbed, people report more headaches, pain, illness, anxiety, and poor self-image. Generally, eight hours of uninterrupted sleep is adequate. If you feel tired upon waking, you may need more sleep; on the other hand, if you wake up feeling good after, say seven hours, then that may be sufficient for you.

If you have trouble sleeping you may find it helpful to:

- Try to develop a regular sleep schedule that is the same at horse shows and at home. Also, try to take a short nap between 1.00 and 3.00 p.m. Try practising the horse show sleep schedule regularly so that your biological clock will become accustomed to it.
- Avoid foods or drinks containing alcohol or caffeine in the latter part of the day because they interfere with natural sleep cycles.
- Eat small, low-fat dinners that include protein.
- If you feel 'wound-up' before bed, try developing a relaxing ritual, such as reading before bed, meditation, yoga, or listening to soft music. This provides a period of transition and may help you sleep more easily.
- Do not eat or work in your bedroom; it should be a place for sleep.
- When you have difficulty falling asleep, get out of bed, go to another room and try to relax. If your mind is racing, write down what you are thinking about. Return to bed when you feel more relaxed.

Remember, sleep plays as crucial a role in training as does hard work! Its effects are mental and physical.

NUTRITION

Nutrition is another vital aspect of training for peak performance. What riders eat for meals and snacks, and when they eat, can have a major impact on performance. Riders need to eat well-balanced diets. Meal schedules are important because the nutrients provide the energy for performance. While nervousness and hectic schedules often prevent riders from eating properly, the truth is that eating regularly may actually help reduce nervousness and provide more energy to cope with busy schedules. Five small meals per day may be more effective than three large ones, especially on long show days; this schedule will help maintain consistent blood sugar levels and energy levels, and contribute to a sense of well-being. Eating only one or two meals per day will not provide the kind of energy needed to perform well.

In hot weather, the body actually needs more energy for performance than in cooler weather. So, although appetite may be reduced during hot weather, remember that the need to maintain energy levels will not be.

The nutritional needs of riders will differ according to the amount of exercise that they get each day. In general, nutritional needs depend on factors such as the length and intensity of the exercise and the amount of energy expended (the demands of the sport), weather conditions, and the individual's own metabolism.

What to Eat

Current research recommends that a healthy diet consists of 30 per cent fat (10 per cent saturated, 10 per cent monounsaturated, and 10 per cent polyunsaturated); 12 per cent protein, and 58 per cent carbohydrates (48 per cent complex carbohydrates and naturally occurring sugars and 10 per cent refined and processed sugars). Riders need diets that are rich in carbohydrates, supplemented with protein. Professionals who ride for several hours a day may want to increase their protein intake above 12 per cent because of their endurance energy requirements. Foods which are rich in complex carbohydrates and naturally occurring sugars include: potatoes, rice, whole grains, beans, fruits, and vegetables.

These foods, rich in vitamins and minerals, provide steady energy for many hours. For riders who feel that it is too hot to eat such foods, or that they are too heavy to digest, or for riders whose stomachs are too 'nervous', there are carbohydrate-rich, nutritionally sound 'meal replacement' sports drinks available, usually through health food stores.

Simple carbohydrates include: sucrose, fructose, dextrose, maltose, corn sweetener, corn syrup, sorghum, sorbital, honey, and white sugar. Simple carbohydrates 'sweeten up' our lives but give us very little long-term energy for riding. When ingested on an empty stomach they raise blood sugar levels temporarily, but then cause them to drop to low levels. Low blood sugar has a negative effect on performance because it reduces brain and muscle function. The effects of low blood sugar include headache, nervousness, inability to concentrate, and fatigue. Therefore, riders should not ingest large amounts of simple carbohydrates for breakfast (because of the fast during sleep), or on an otherwise empty stomach. For example, sugary cereals, doughnuts, pastries or candy bars on an empty stomach will give a temporary energy boost, but will then usually cause an even larger drop in energy.

Proteins include: meat, poultry, fish, eggs, and milk products. Plant proteins include: legumes, whole grains, pasta, rice, and seeds. Proteins build and repair muscle tissue; they help regulate chemical balance and are involved in the formation of hormones, antibodies and enzymes; they also supply energy when carbohydrates are not available.

Saturated fats are animal fats – they elevate blood cholesterol levels. Vegetable oils are generally polyunsaturated and monounsaturated fats. However, avoid hydrogenated vegetable oils, which are saturated fats. Fats provide twice the energy that carbohydrates and proteins provide. They are digested slowly, and supply energy for the growth of skin; transport fat-soluble vitamins; and help regulate hormones.

Sample Horse Show Meal Plan

Upon rising
Three ounces of fruit juice

Breakfast
Two eggs
Wholewheat toast, English or bran muffin, or bagel
Fresh fruit
Handful of raw almonds
    or
Cooked cereal (oatmeal or cream of wheat) with milk
Fresh fruit

Mid-morning snack
One piece of fresh fruit; or a handful of nuts; or a bagel; or 12 ounces of V-8 juice; or orange or grapefruit juice (1 part) diluted with 2 parts water; or slice of wholewheat bread with peanut butter; or museli mixed with diluted orange juice

Lunch
Large salad with chicken or tuna, one piece of fresh fruit; or hamburger, grilled chicken, tuna or fish sandwich, fruit; or large bowl of vegetable, mushroom, pea, or lentil soup (no cream soups), fresh fruit

Mid-afternoon snack
Same as mid-morning snack

Dinner
Broiled or grilled chicken, fish, or lean meat, cooked vegetables, salad, fresh fruit, one slice of wholegrain bread.

After-dinner snack
Same as mid-morning snack

Because of the showing schedule you may have to interchange snack and meal times. This is a general idea of the type of nutrition needed for peak performance. Liquid carbohydrate replacement drinks may also be substituted for snacks. Meals should be eaten at least forty-five minutes before performing.

HYDRATION

Hydration is fluid replacement for the body. Important during any season, it becomes even more crucial during hot weather. Water is the ultimate source of hydration and it needs to be consumed in small amounts all day long – not just after performance. Fluid replacement drinks work best if diluted with water. They contain a high sugar content, which can actually dehydrate the body cells rather than rehydrate them. Especially in hot weather, this can cause nausea. Diluting these drinks with water corrects this problem. Mixing water with orange, grapefruit or cranberry juice makes another healthy sports drink. In general, drinks that contain caffeine, alcohol or sugar tend to dehydrate rather than hydrate, causing drops in energy and interfering with recovery from exercise.

Surprising though it may seem, thirst is not a good indicator of dehydration. Dehydration causes feelings of lethargy, fatigue and exhaustion – and is associated with heat exhaustion and heat-stroke. Even when it is not hot, drinking plenty of water will help maintain your energy level and help you to recover from strenuous exercise.

ALCOHOL AND PERFORMANCE

The effects of alcohol differ from person to person, and depend on factors such as mood, time of day, whether ingested on a full or empty stomach, and (in women) time in menstrual cycle. Alcohol acts as a central nervous system depressant and has a rebound effect;

moreover, it can interfere with the natural feelings of balance, since it physiologically and psychologically takes you on a roller-coaster from high to low, continuing to rebound in that manner until the body regains its homeostasis. Consuming more than 3–6 ounces of alcohol per day can affect the development of consistent, high level performance, because the mind and body can not be balanced and consistent when rebounding and/or dehydrated from the alcohol.

As a method of controlling nerves, alcohol is ineffective in the long run because the body develops a tolerance to alcohol and then a dependency upon it. Once a tolerance develops, more alcohol is required to produce the desired effect of relaxation, which can lead to alcoholism. Drinking whilst performing can also be quite dangerous because of the perceptual alterations, dulled reaction times and misjudgements produced by alcohol.

Riders need to get to the root cause of the issue. Masking symptoms such as nerves with a substance such as alcohol can only lead to disaster. Riding a horse is like driving a car: sooner or later substance abuse will catch up with you. Riders who are unwilling to consider the risk to themselves should consider the well-being of their partner, the horse.

Putting it all together. Mental and physical training, good nutrition and a great equine partner will make your dreams come true. The author and her faithful partner *Bye Farr*.

Conclusion

Now that you have read through this book and completed the exercises, give yourself a big pat on the back. You have learned how to incorporate mental training into your training as a rider. By completing the book you have shown the mental persistence and commitment that will enable you to become the best rider that you can be. Remember, focus in the present; think positively; develop solutions to your problems in a relaxed manner; concentrate on what you do right, how you want to perform; and be patient. Allow yourself to have fun and enjoy the journey that your riding career takes you on.

As a sport psychologist, the great joy for me is watching clients overcome the obstacles that get in the way of their success and discover the potential that is within. I use the basic skills that have been presented in this book and suggest that the riders develop good, solid, riding skills. Armed with the mental and physical knowledge and skills, and willing equine partners, I have watched my clients make their dreams come true. Best of luck on your quest to become the best rider that you can be!

References

Bunker, L.B., Rotella, R., & Reilly, A. (eds.) *Sport Psychology: Psychological Considerations for Maximizing Sport Performance*, (Ithaca, New York, Mouvement Publications 1985).

Gawain, S., *Creative Visualization Workbook*, (New York, Bantam Books 1985).

Greene, M., *personal communication*.

Holtz, L., Videotape, (Washington, Washington Speakers Bureau).

Kursinski, A., *Anne Kursinski's Riding and Jumping Clinic*, (New York, Doubleday 1995).

Newman, K., *personal communication*.

Oxendine, J.B., 'Emotional arousal and motor performance', *Quest*, vol. 13, (1970), pp.23–32.

Ravizza, K., Peak experiences in sport, *Journal of Humanistic Psychlogy*, 17, (1977), pp.35–40.

Rotella, R.J., *personal communication*.

Rotella, R.J. & Coop, R., *Golfing Out of Your Mind* (Audiotape), (Charlottesville, Virginia, Creative Media Productions 1985).

Index

control strategies *110*
coping script 80–2
past events 13–14
see also concentration; focus of
  attention
doubts *see* negative thinking
dressage test
  memorizing 97
  peak performance curve 9
  three-day event 101–2
  worksheet *107*
drinks 122–3

effectiveness, learned 53–4
energy levels
  during a course 99
  for peak performance 8–9
errors
  accepting 10
  and perfectionism 42–3
event *see* three-day event
excuses 33

fatigue 50–1, 117–18, 121
Fischer, Craig 33
focus of attention 84–6
  developing 87–9, 95
  in dressage test 102
focus on present 13–15, 43
  attaining 11, 14–15
  and errors 9–11
  questionnaire 15–16
focus on process 59–61
frustration
  causes 113–14
  dealing with 114–16

Gawain, Shakti 67
goals 61–2
  doubts about 32, 67
  effective 62
  examples of setting 63–5

obstacles to 66–7
setting new 68
visualizing 67, 71–2

Holtz, Lou 27
honesty, with self 25–6
humour 50
hydration 122

Ingold, Michelle *28*
innovation, openness to 24
instinct, rider's 41
instructor 42

Jefferson, Thomas 25
jumps
  horse's dislike of 106
  'huge' 105
  spooky 105–6

Keeney, Jessie *115*
Kursinski, Anne 104, 112

learned effectiveness 53–4
'let down' 33, 68
Lufkin, Abigail 86–7

mastery and coping rehearsal 72–4
  audiotapes 60, 73
  coping script 80–2
  list for mastery script 73–4
  mastery script 75–80
motivation 37
  balancing 54–6
  learned effectiveness 53–4
  and negative thinking 17–18
  perfectionism 40
  underachievement 51–3

negative thinking 17–18
  and goals 67
  tuning out 20–1

798.2   Reilly, Ann S.
        A sport psychology
     workbook for riders.